Cambridge
Primary Reading
Anthologies 6

Student's Book
with Online Audio

Scope and Sequence

Unit 1 What makes your region unique?

	Genre	Key Words	Reading Strategy
Fiction *Under the Banyan*	Realistic Fiction	gigantic, thrive, loose, resemble, unwelcome, cricket, forbid, sympathize, refuse, diverse	Identifying Setting
Nonfiction *Working in the Coldest Place on Earth*	Magazine Profile of Environmental Scientists	board (v), dock, iceberg, bow, crew, descend, thaw, blizzard, elevation, desolate	Comparing and Contrasting

Unit 2 Why do we seek adventure?

	Genre	Key Words	Reading Strategy
Fiction *I'm Fairly Fond of Flying, Today I Rode a Thrill Ride,* and *I Found a Buried-Treasure Map*	Poetry	fond of, land (v), thrill, panic (v), pump (v), race (v), terrifying, blast, quest, pleasure	Asking Questions
Nonfiction *Getting Out of the Comfort Zone*	Adventure Camp Diary	adventurous, first aid, zone, exhausting, ascend, cliff, intense, rapids, sprain (v), limit	Identifying Point of View

Unit 3 How can we understand a work of art?

	Genre	Key Words	Reading Strategy
Fiction *Rembrandt's Apprentice*	Historical Fiction	destiny, stack, brilliant, admire, magnificent, unattractive, glance (v), exclaim, imposing, toss	Analyzing Characters
Nonfiction *Art Blog: Why Should You See Art in Person?*	Opinion Blog on the Arts	surround, pause (v), rewarding, appreciate, etiquette, distraction, scale, subtle, convey, mane	Annotating

Unit 4 How does information technology shape our lives?

	Genre	Key Words	Reading Strategy
Fiction *Reality Lost*	Science Fiction	startle, virtual, labyrinth, disturb, blink (v), solitary, gaze, wander, gasp (v), thrust (v)	Identifying Point of View
Nonfiction *Will Robots Replace Humans?*	Magazine Article on Technology	slang, fluent, artificial intelligence, streaming, navigation, tedious, alert (v), diagnose, recall (v), preference	Drawing Conclusions

Unit 5 How can we save the planet?

	Genre	Key Words	Reading Strategy
Fiction *All the Way into the City*	Realistic Fiction	rally, approve of, distrust, watch over, reusable, overreact, irritate, air quality, atmosphere, limp (v)	Predicting and Setting a Purpose for Reading
Nonfiction *Take Steps to Reduce Your Carbon Footprint and Save the Planet*	Expert Interviews	threaten, scarcity, substitute (v), decrease, reliance, disposable, biodegradable, particle, trendy, distinctive	Rereading

Unit 6 What makes a good story?

	Genre	Key Words	Reading Strategy
Fiction *A Hairy Situation*	Fantasy Movie Script	exterior, lobby, skyscraper, engrossed, flutter (v), trapped, gust, interior, flight of stairs, stairwell	Identifying Literary Genres
Nonfiction *Scary Fairies: Should Fairy Tales Be Frightening?*	Magazine Article on the Arts	cottage, porridge, troll, series, dire, illustration, property, obey, overcome, persuade	Identifying Text Structure

Unit 7 Why do we need medicine?

	Genre	Key Words	Reading Strategy
Fiction *The Racing Pulse*	Realistic Fiction	pulse, massage (v), suspect (v), gracefully, sulk, perceive, acupuncture, defiant, coma, enthusiastic	Synthesizing
Nonfiction *Antibiotics of the Future?*	Biological Sciences Report	effective, widespread, theorize, annually, microbiologist, industry, frigid, waterproof, technique, medieval	Identifying Cause and Effect

Unit 8 How do we use money?

	Genre	Key Words	Reading Strategy
Fiction *Woogle Zoo*	Graphic Novel	ordeal, novice, expert, disheartened, industrious, set up (v), infuriating, ridiculous, imaginary, request (v)	Identifying Theme
Money Makes the World Go Around	Informational Text on Social Studies	earn, barter, value, stamp (v), vault, receipt, issue (v), raised, metallic, currency	Quoting from a Text

Unit 9 How can we increase our brainpower?

	Genre	Key Words	Reading Strategy
Fiction *The Mystery at the School Fair*	Mystery	nickname, reminder, slightly, confirm, vaguely, coincidence, speculate, scold, gossip (v), hideous	Monitoring and Clarifying
Nonfiction *What Kind of Genius Are You?*	Personality Quiz	genius, figure out, intelligence, joke, versatile, playlist, visualize, detailed, perspective, cheer up	Synthesizing

1 What makes your region unique?

Key Words

1 🎧 **Preview the Key Words.**
1.1

gigantic   thrive   loose   resemble   unwelcome

cricket   forbid   sympathize   refuse   diverse

2 **Read the definitions and write the Key Words.**

a including many differences _____

b to grow happily and healthily _____

c to be similar to someone or something _____

d to be kind and show you understand _____

e to not allow someone to do something _____

f to say that you will not do something _____

Pre-reading

3 🗣 **Look at the illustrations in the story and make predictions.**

Setting for *Under the Banyan*

Place (region, urban/rural) _____

Historical Time (past/present/future) _____

Weather _____

Landscape _____

4 🎧 **Listen and read.**
1.2

Under the Banyan

By Lucy Pawlak • Illustrated by Kathia Recio

Gayatri sweeps around the roots of the banyan tree. She has been sweeping all day, but she's not even halfway around it. It will take four days of hard work. Gayatri isn't slow or lazy. She is 76 years old, but she can still work hard and move fast. It will take Gayatri four days because the banyan is gigantic. The tree has thousands of hanging roots that stretch down from the branches and into the ground. From far away, it looks like a forest, but really it is just one tree. The shade of the banyan spreads over an area bigger than a soccer field. There are banyan trees like this all across India. The widest tree in the world is a banyan. It covers almost 2,000 square meters and is about 550 years old.

Gayatri lives in the shade of the banyan tree, on the edge of the rural town of Kalipi in South India. She takes good care of the tree because the tree has taken good care of her. Gayatri has been taking care of it for over 40 years. She found the great banyan tree when she was walking alone in the forest. Her family had moved far away to the north, so she was feeling sad. She saw that the tree was weak and needed to be taken care of. Near its trunk, she built a small cabin where she could sleep. To this day she has never left the tree. It has thrived, growing healthy and strong with her help. These days, the cabin is a little bit dusty and many of the clay sculptures are broken. Gayatri knows it needs to be cleaned and painted, but she is getting old, and she can't do everything.

Today Gayatri's friend Sumona is helping her sweep. Sometimes they stop to tie small bags of soil to roots that do not reach the ground so that the tree will be well fed. Sometimes they put wet clay between the roots that reach into the ground so that they do not become loose. Sumona is an artist; she loves to photograph banyan trees. Sumona and Gayatri are working on a project. They meet to take photos and tell the story of life under the banyan tree. Gayatri worries about who will look after it when she is too old. She is happy that Sumona understands the importance of the tree.

For some people, banyans are the tree of life because they can live for hundreds of years. They are home to many insects and animals. Each part of the tree is used for making different medicines. Other people believe it's actually the tree of death because nothing grows under it and banyans are often found close to graveyards. And other people think the tree's long hanging roots resemble the hair of a wise old man. Gayatri likes the fairy tale about the tree being like a mother: once upon a time, a banyan saved two babies, who had been left alone in its shade, by feeding them its milk-like sap. Caring for this banyan has given Gayatri a home in this place.

Now many visitors make long journeys to visit the tree. Gayatri enjoys showing them around and sharing her knowledge, but recently, like today, there have been some unwelcome guests. Gayatri and Sumona, sweeping around the tree, hear a crack and then cheering and laughter. Gayatri peers through the vegetation. The kids from the village are playing cricket under the tree. The ball cracks against a root. "Out!" They cry. Gayatri is furious; she hates to see them harm her poor banyan!

Arjun got the cricket bat for his birthday. Ever since, he has been playing nonstop with his friends. It's too hot in the sun, so they play in the shade of the great banyan tree. The spot is perfect, except for the angry old woman who lives there. They call her Mrs. Angry because she is always shouting and interfering with their fun. The kids play in the afternoon, when Mrs. Angry is napping. They chose their spot carefully, as far away as possible from where she sleeps. The children love playing cricket in the shade. They practice all the time and are becoming very good. They decide to make a club and name it after the tree. They paint a beautiful sign along a branch that reads "Banyan Junior Cricket Club."

The day that Gayatri and Sumona decide to sweep around the banyan is an important day for the Banyan Junior Cricket Club. Arjun and his friends are playing their first official match. When Gayatri and Sumona look through the roots to see who is cheering, they are surprised to see more then 20 children. Sumona turns to Gayatri to ask her what is going on and is surprised to see the old woman is transforming: her face is becoming very red, and her eyes seem to be on fire. Gayatri is as frightening as a great tiger; she has turned into Mrs. Angry. Sumona watches as Mrs. Angry runs out into the center of the game, shouting: "What is the meaning of this? I have forbidden you to play cricket under my tree!" The children are frightened and silent. Just then, Mrs. Angry sees the sign they have painted on the branch. "You have even attacked my tree with graffiti! Get out! Go! Or I will call the police!" she shouts. Sumona is surprised; she has never seen Gayatri behave like this before.

After the children have left, Sumona takes the old lady back home for a cup of calming tea. She slowly turns back into the Gayatri who Sumona knows and loves. Sumona feels sorry for her, but she also sympathizes with the children. They looked so happy playing cricket, and the sign they painted was original and colorful.

The following day, Sumona decides to look for the children and get their side of the story. She finds Arjun and his friends playing cricket in the hot sun that afternoon. Arjun tells her about the Banyan Junior Cricket Club and Mrs. Angry who refuses to let them play.

"Why is she so mean to us? We just want to play cricket in the cool shade of the tree! The tree is big enough for all of us!"

"Yes," agrees Sumona. "The tree is big enough for everyone."

Sumona can see Arjun's point, but she also thinks the children should respect the banyan tree. She knows that, when Gayatri's family left her, she put all her love into the tree. She sees herself as the protector of the tree. Sumona walks among the hanging roots thinking about a way to solve the problem. "Help me banyan tree," she says aloud. "After all, maybe there's a way you can benefit, too!"

She stops and looks around; she has reached Gayatri's little cabin near the center of the tree. Clay models of people as well as animals and bowls are displayed all around. Many of them are broken and everything is very dirty and in need of paint. Sumona wipes mud off a clay horse and has a great idea—it's a long shot, but it might just work.

Three weeks have passed, and Sumona's plan is working perfectly. The faded, dusty little cabin has been transformed; it is clean and freshly painted. Gayatri is nearby having her afternoon nap, and not much further off are Arjun and the entire Banyan Junior Cricket Club. They are sweeping around the banyan; they greet Sumona happily and ask her if she would like to join them for cricket practice later.

These days the cricket club helps Gayatri, they re-paint the clay animals and people and take care of the surrounding flora and fauna in the forest. In return, they can continue to play cricket in the banyan's shade. They have grown to love the tree too, so caring for it is not a chore. If everyone respects the banyan, there should be no reason why they cannot all enjoy its huge umbrella of shade, its endlessly expanding branches, its deep roots, and its diverse worlds.

Key Words

1 **Complete the sentences with the Key Words.**

| refuse | unwelcome | cricket | forbid | loose | thrive | gigantic |

a Most plants and trees need water and sunlight in order to _____.

b You need a bat and ball to play _____. It resembles baseball, but it's not the same!

c The widest tree in the world is a _____ banyan tree.

d We need to protect the tree from _____ beetles that attack the roots.

e Many children _____ to eat broccoli because they don't like how it tastes.

f I think I need to go to the dentist because one of my teeth is _____. I can feel it moving!

g The rules of soccer _____ everyone except the goalie from using their hands.

Comprehension

2 **Circle the correct options to complete the summary.**

The story *Under the Banyan* has a happy ending, but the tone is kind of **angry / sad / frightening**. This is because Gayatri's cabin is **old and dirty / clean and colorful**, and she is not able to take care of the tree on her own. The tree is very important to Gayatri and the community, and she gets **frightened / worried / angry** when people treat it badly. However, her friend Sumona has a **bad / good / silly** idea for how everyone can benefit from the tree.

3 **Write the information.**

a Two things Gayatri and Sumona do to take care of the tree:

_____

_____

b Two things people call the banyan tree:

_____

_____

c Two changes to Gayatri's face when she gets angry:

_____

_____

d Two things the children do to help:

_____

_____

Digging Deeper

4 **Answer the questions.**

a Why do you think Gayatri values the banyan so much?

_____

_____

b Why have Gayatri and Sumona become friends?

_____

_____

c Why do the children playing cricket under the banyan tree make Gayatri so angry?

_____

_____

d How does the sign give Sumona an idea?

_____

_____

5 **Write notes in the graphic organizer.**

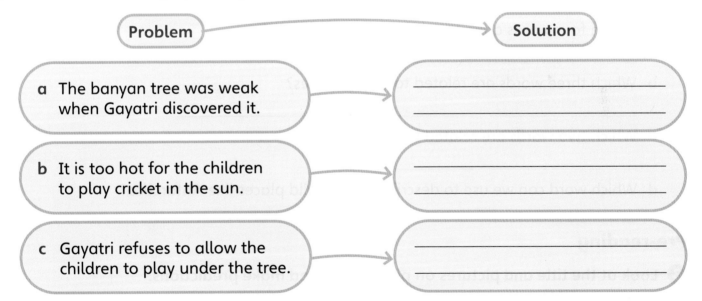

Problem ⟶ Solution

a The banyan tree was weak when Gayatri discovered it.

_____
_____

b It is too hot for the children to play cricket in the sun.

_____
_____

c Gayatri refuses to allow the children to play under the tree.

_____
_____

Personalization

6 **Think about a unique or important feature in the area where you live (human-made or natural). Write notes in the chart.**

Unique Feature	
Things the Community Can Do to Protect It	

What makes your region unique?

Key Words

1 🎧 **Preview the Key Words.**
1.3

| board (v) | dock | iceberg | bow | crew |

| descend | thaw | blizzard | elevation | desolate |

2 Answer the questions with the Key Words.

a   Which four words are related to boats and sailing?

_____ _____ _____ _____

b   Which three words are related to cold climates?

_____ _____ _____

c   Which two words are related to height?

_____ _____

d   Which word can we use to describe empty, wild places like Antarctica?

_____

Pre-reading

3 Look at the title and pictures on pages 13–15 and make predictions.

a   What is the weather like in this place? _____

b   What wildlife lives there? _____

c   Where is this place? _____

d   What clothes do people wear? _____

e   What food do they eat? _____

f   What jobs do people do? _____

g   Do people live in this place for long periods of time? _____

4 🎧 **Listen and read.**
1.4

Working in the Coldest Place on Earth

Antarctica, the coldest and windiest place on Earth, is also the only continent in the world with no permanent population. However, there are about 82 scientific stations from 32 countries set up there. Every year, scientists visit these stations to research climate change's effect on Antarctica.

Can you imagine what it's like to live there? I was in Antarctica for a year, so come with me to find out what it's like in the coldest place on Earth!

Doing research in Antarctica

Getting There

After we board the ship, we wave farewell to our families on the dock. Five days later, we hear someone shouting, "Iceberg!" That's the first evidence that we are coming close to Antarctica.

Finally, 25 days after we left Australia, our ship blows its horn three times to signal we have arrived at the research station. We stand on the bow of the ship and look at the landscape. We spot Adélie penguins warming themselves in the sunshine, and sleepy leopard seals raise their heads as if to say hello.

We are greeted by the people at the station. They are happy to see us because we bring food, fuel, and gifts from home. After a couple of days, the old group will return home, and we will stay here with the new crew of 30.

Fall

It's only February, but in Antarctica it's nearly fall—time to plan our two-month expedition. Packing and getting the vehicles ready requires help from everyone, including the carpenter, electrician, mechanic, doctor, and cook. Six of us, mostly scientists, will go on the journey.

We head south using four tractor trains and three bulldozers. The sleds carry our food supplies. After traveling many kilometers, we descend into a valley where we will measure wind patterns.

Survival means staying covered by two or three layers of clothes because wind can freeze your skin instantly. We also need to do whatever it takes to stay warm, such as doing jumping jacks or covering ourselves in blankets—inside the vehicles!

When May approaches, we go back to the station.

Winter

Sea ice starting to form

Winter here is so cold that the surface of the ocean turns to ice. Saltwater freezes at a lower temperature (about -2 °C) than fresh water, and the sea ice won't thaw until summer arrives. Power might fail when the wind reaches over 200 km/h. Fortunately, we have a tunnel to connect the buildings during blizzards.

This is the most difficult time of the year. It's especially hard because no ships or planes come. Also, we can't go more than a few kilometers from the station. The winds carry the dense, cold air from the higher elevations in the center of Antarctica. They can cause violent snowstorms that make it very dangerous to stay outside.

June, in particular, is challenging. It's the month with the longest and coldest nights (-30 °C).

So, on June 21, the shortest day of the year, we organize a midwinter party. We decorate the station with flags, balloons, and lights. We congratulate each other and eat a special meal prepared by our cook. We also perform an Antarctic version of *Cinderella*. Most important, we receive electronic cards from around the world, from loved ones, leaders, and even strangers. These cards remind us that we have friends around the world waiting for us to return home!

A snowstorm

Spring

We are planning a four-month journey in the spring, so the cook is baking three hundred loaves of bread for the team! In September, we leave the station, excited for a new season of light. We will install a wind turbine. This way of generating energy is not only good for the planet, but it is also the most reliable way to make electricity in Antarctica!

Work is fine, but we miss being in contact with other living beings. We are in the middle of nowhere, and the only thing we see around us is ice. It's desolate. However, there's nothing like the spectacular views at midnight.

A new wind turbine

Summer

Finally, it gets warmer—nearly 15 °C! This is the best time of the year to study Antarctica's fauna. We travel to a nearby island to study the Antarctic petrel, the seabird that lives on the islands of Antarctica. They usually nest on rocks or under boulders. We are concerned that some species are decreasing in population, so we record our findings.

As we do our work, the Adélie penguins get very curious and come close, while the seals completely ignore us. It astonishes us how sociable some creatures are or are not!

As we return to the station, after our work is done, we spot in the distance an island where royal penguins are camping. What a beautiful sight! They are disappearing because of global warming. We also discover some elephant seals and notice whales in the distance.

This is the perfect ending to our year in Antarctica. We are ready to go home. It will be nice to wear only one layer of clothing for a while!

Royal penguins

Antarctic petrels

15

Key Words

1 Write the Key Words that match the definitions.

a _____: a large, floating mass of ice from a glacier

b _____: to become warmer and melt

c _____: a windy snowstorm

d _____: the front of a ship

e _____: height above Earth's surface

f _____: having no people, plants, or animals

g _____: to get onto a ship, boat, or airplane

Comprehension

2 Circle *T* (true) or *F* (false).

a	People live permanently in Antarctica.	T	F
b	The writer boarded the ship in Australia.	T	F
c	In the fall, everyone at the research station travels south.	T	F
d	There is no communication with families during winter.	T	F
e	The wind turbine is a not a good source of electricity.	T	F
f	Adélie penguins are not very sociable.	T	F

3 Compare and contrast the seasons. Use the information in the text to complete the chart. (If there is no information, leave the field blank.)

	Fall	Winter	Spring	Summer
Weather				
Food				
Work				

Digging Deeper

4 **Answer the questions.**

a Why is the summer the best time of the year to study animals in Antarctica?

_____

_____

b Why is the winter the most dangerous time of the year in Antarctica?

_____

_____

c How do you think Antarctica might change if global warming gets worse?

_____

_____

5 **Read what the scientists might say and write the corresponding season.**

a "I haven't seen anyone except my team members for over three months. I can't wait to get back to the research station. But the night sky is beautiful!"

_____

c "It is more comfortable at this time of the year, but we're a little worried. It is even warmer than usual, and there are fewer animals than last year."

_____

b "The cook did a great job. We didn't expect such a huge meal. At the end of the party, we received a message from Australia's prime minister!"

_____

d "I haven't been here long, and I wasn't expecting the wind to be so strong in the valley. I'm glad I packed plenty of layers to stay warm!"

_____

Personalization

6 **Imagine you are on a year-long trip to Antarctica. Choose a season and write an email to a friend to say what you are doing and how you feel.**

New Message
_____
_____
_____
_____
_____

2 Why do we seek adventure?

Key Words

1   **Preview the Key Words.**
2.1

 fond of

 land (v)

 thrill

 panic (v)

 pump (v)

 race (v)

 terrifying

 blast

 quest

 pleasure

2 **Match the Key Words to their synonyms.**

1	fond of	a	a feeling of happiness
2	thrill	b	scary
3	terrifying	c	to go very fast
4	quest	d	to arrive on the ground
5	panic	e	like
6	race	f	excitement
7	pleasure	g	a search for something
8	land	h	to suddenly feel afraid

Pre-reading

3 **Look at the pictures on pages 19–21 and write notes in the chart.**

Poem	How the Characters Feel	Why
a "I'm Fairly Fond of Flying"		
b "Today I Rode a Thrill Ride"		
c "I Found a Buried-Treasure Map"		

4  **Listen and read.**
2.2

I'm Fairly Fond of Flying

By Kenn Nesbitt • Illustrated by Ricardo Figueroa

I'm fairly fond of flying.
Yes, flying's fun to do.
I fly for all my holidays
and each vacation, too.

I'll take a trip to Turkey,
or Poland, or Peru.
I'll hop a plane to France or Spain,
or even Timbuktu.

I never take a taxi.
I never sail a ship.
I never hike or ride a bike
to travel on a trip.

And when the plane has landed,
I run right out the door.
It's fun to fly; however, I
like landing even more.

Today I Rode a Thrill Ride

By Kenn Nesbitt • Illustrated by Ricardo Figueroa

Today I rode a thrill ride
that was totally extreme.
It made me start to panic.
It made me start to scream.

My adrenaline was pumping
and my heart began to race
from sheer exhilaration
and the wind that whipped my face.

It bounced and bumped and banged
at such a terrifying speed
that, when the ride was over,
I was utterly weak-kneed.

I thought it was impossible
for rides to go that fast,
but this one was electrifying;
I had such a blast.

It took my breath away
to be on such a thrilling ride.
That rocking horse was awesome!
Next, I think I'll try the slide.

I Found a Buried-Treasure Map

By Kenn Nesbitt • Illustrated by Ricardo Figueroa

I found a buried-treasure map.
I showed it to my brother.
He showed it to our sister,
and she showed it to our mother.

Mom gave our dad the treasure map.
He said, "We'll start a quest
to find the gold and silver
in that ancient pirate's chest."

So we became adventurers
and sailed the seven seas,
exploring every country
from Botswana to Belize.

At last we reached the "X" mark
and discovered, to our pleasure,
our home is where the riches are.
Our family is the treasure.

Key Words

1 Complete the text with the correct form of the Key Words.

thrill	land	pump	blast	pleasure	panic	fond of	terrifying

I had a **(a)** _____ on my last vacation! It was so much fun!

I visited my cousins, who I'm very **(b)** _____. It gives me a lot of

(c) _____ to spend time with them. We went to an amusement park and

rode on a brand new **(d)** _____ ride. It didn't frighten me at all. However,

I did get frightened on the flight back. While the plane was **(e)** _____,

there was a huge thunderstorm. It was **(f)** _____! When the plane finally

touched the ground, it bounced a few times. I didn't **(g)** _____, but I could

feel that my heart was **(h)** _____ really fast! I was glad to get off the

plane and into a taxi. The ride from the airport to our house felt much safer.

Comprehension

2 Read the sentences and write if they refer to "I'm Fairly Fond of Flying" (*FFF*), "Today I Rode a Thrill Ride" (*TR*), or "I Found a Buried-Treasure Map" (*BTM*).

a The characters search all over the world for something. _____

b The narrator prefers one form of transportation over all others. _____

c It was hard for the narrator to stand up after his/her experience. _____

d Although it was a scary experience, the person really enjoyed it. _____

e The adventure ended at home. _____

f The end of the journey is even better than the journey itself. _____

3 Write notes in the chart.

Poem	Form of Transportation	Reason for Using It
a "I'm Fairly Fond of Flying"		
b "Today I Rode a Thrill Ride"		
c "I Found a Buried-Treasure Map"		

Digging Deeper

4 📖 **Choose one poem from pages 19–21 and answer the questions.**

a Who is the poem about? _____

b What is the setting of the poem? _____

c What happens at the end of the poem? _____

d What is the tone of the poem? _____

e What is the author's purpose for writing the poem? _____

5 **Read the poems again and write notes in the charts.**

	The Poem's Message	
"I'm Fairly Fond of Flying"	"Today I Rode a Thrill Ride"	"I Found a Buried-Treasure Map"

	Lines from the Poem That Convey the Message	
"I'm Fairly Fond of Flying"	"Today I Rode a Thrill Ride"	"I Found a Buried-Treasure Map"

6 **What theme do all three poems share?** _____

Personalization

7 **Choose your favorite poem from pages 19–21. How does it make you feel? Why?**

_____

_____

_____

8 **Write another stanza for your favorite poem.**

_____

_____

_____

_____

(2) Why do we seek adventure?

Key Words

1 **Preview the Key Words.**
2.3

adventurous   first aid   zone   exhausting   ascend

cliff   intense   rapids   sprain (v)   limit

2 Match the sentences.

1 You'll need to wear a life jacket on the boat.

2 This hike is exhausting.

3 There is a 500-meter drop behind you.

4 We need to ascend 100 more meters.

5 He loves climbing and kayaking.

6 This is a litter-free zone.

7 The hills are outside the limits of the city.

a So they are in a rural area.

b So don't go near the edge of the cliff.

c So please take all your garbage with you.

d The rapids are deep and dangerous.

e Then, we'll be at the top of the mountain.

f He's very adventurous.

g We've been walking for hours.

Pre-reading

3 📖 **Look at pages 25–29 and answer the questions.**

a What type of text is it? _____

b Is it written in the first, second, or third person? _____

c Why do you think it is written using this point of view?

_____

4 🎧 **Listen and read.**
2.4

Getting Out of the Comfort Zone

June 10: Off We Go!

When I walked out of school after our final exams, it was a great feeling. Summer vacation! Time to relax and watch videos for the next six weeks, I thought. But I wouldn't be that lucky! Mom and Dad told me that I was going to be spending my first week of summer at an adventure camp.

I'm Kacey. Welcome to My Blog!

"A what?" I asked, not believing my own ears.

"An adventure camp—you know, a place where you get to spend a week in the wilderness, kayaking, backpacking, rock climbing, sleeping outside in a tent," Dad explained.

"You've been stuck in your room for two months, and a little adventure will be good for you," Mom added.

"Do I have a choice?" I asked.

I didn't, and, before I knew it, I was packing my bags (including this laptop I'm writing on) for a so-called adventure. I decided to do some research before we left. The center is in the Lake District, where, obviously, there are a lot of lakes. But there are rivers, mountains, and forests, too. It looked beautiful, but was it going to be as fun as six weeks in front of a screen? Definitely not!

Please don't misunderstand me—I love adventure, and I think it's a great thing for some people. When we were younger, my brother, Mom, Dad, and I would go camping a few times a year, and we've always loved outdoor activities. I've known how to read a map and use a compass since I was seven, too. People always say how important it is to be adventurous, and I'm happy they feel that way. I just don't want to be adventurous this time.

Our destination: the Lake District of Northern England

Wish me luck!

June 11: The Uncomfortable Zone

It's the end of my first day, and it was actually more fun than I expected. I'm writing this on my phone (I couldn't take my laptop) while I sit outside a tent in some sand dunes by the beach.

Molly on the long hike to the beach

Dad dropped me off yesterday, and I met the instructors, Jed and Emma, and the other adventurers; there are six of us in total. They seem really friendly. Molly and I got along immediately. (Now we're sharing this tent!) After that, we did a few (boring) activities to get to know each other as well as some basic first-aid training, which I don't think we'll need. Then, we had to say why we were here, and I admitted that my parents had made me come. Some of the others gave much better answers: Kate said that she wanted a challenge and to learn new things about herself. And Russel said that he wanted to leave his comfort zone, to start doing new things, and to feel more confident in himself.

Is getting out of your comfort zone a good thing? If I told the truth, I'd rather be in my comfort zone. I would rather be doing what I always do: watching another season of my favorite show. Except I'm here camping on the beach—in a beautiful location—after an exhausting day of hiking. There isn't anybody telling me what to do, so that's good, I guess.

Our tent (or "the uncomfortable zone," as I call it) near the beach

June 13: The Danger Zone

What a tough day! We're back at the center now, and everyone is exhausted. I can't believe what we did today.

After camping out all night near the beach, we returned to the center to gather our equipment and supplies for the day. The Lake District is one of the places where rock climbing was invented, so of course we *had* to do it. I've never done it before, but I wasn't that nervous climbing the rock face. What I *was* nervous about was rappelling. That would put me far outside of my comfort zone— right in the middle of the danger zone!

Rappelling is when you descend the rock face you have just ascended using a rope and other equipment. The worst part was the start; it was one of the scariest things I think I've ever done. (I'm a little scared of heights.) You have to lean backward out over the cliff edge and then begin to lower yourself down. You use one hand to slow yourself down and the other to hold on to the rope above you. My legs felt weak the whole way down! It was terrifying but exhilarating, too. When I reached the bottom, the adrenaline rush was intense.

So, even though I was afraid, it all went surprisingly well! I hadn't thought about what might happen to Brad and Betty in the second season of my favorite show once. That's what the danger zone does to you!

Our instructor, Emma, made it look easy.

Jed rapelling

Kayaking on the lake after rappelling

June 17: The Wilderness

We're back at the center now, and it's our last night here at the camp. We spent the past couple of nights out in the wilderness alone. First, we had to find our campsite, but all we were given was a map and a compass—it's called orienteering. I've done it before, and it's fun—but not as much fun in the rain.

Hiking in the rain, me leading the way

It took us most of the day to find our campsite, after we hiked across fields, through rivers, down valleys, and up mountains. It was hard work, and I was a little worried because the only people we could rely on were ourselves. The others were shocked that I could read a real map (Thanks, Mom and Dad!) and were grateful when we finally got to the campsite just before dark. I can't believe I'm saying this, but it's possible that I'm actually enjoying this. I feel a sense of freedom and control over my life that I haven't felt for a while. Marshmallows never tasted so good either!

making dessert

The next day started off well. We went rafting down a river until we reached the point where we had to get on the hiking trail again. Rafting was great, especially going over the rapids, but, it had started to rain again by the time we started hiking. We had to hike up a steep hill, which was rocky, and it was kind of dangerous. Then, Molly slipped and sprained her ankle pretty badly. She was in a lot of pain and could barely walk, so we bandaged her ankle and took turns helping her.

Rafting down the river

"We might need to cut off your leg," joked Russel. Molly didn't think that was funny, but it made us realize that it wasn't as serious as we thought, perhaps because of the first-aid training we had done. (Hopefully, you've forgotten what I said about that a few days ago.) Molly was feeling a lot better by the time we finally reached our campsite again.

The next morning, Jed and Emma were waiting for us when we woke up. They told us that the way we had worked together was great, that we'd come a long way, and that they were proud of us.

Emma asked me, "What happened to the old Kacey?"

I said, "I don't know. Maybe leaving my comfort zone was all I needed to become the Kacey I am now."

June 18: Homeward Bound

Mom and Dad are on their way to pick me up, and Molly has left already, with her foot still in a bandage. We promised to text each other.

I don't want to leave!

Last night, Jed and Emma asked us what *adventure* meant to us. I remember saying something, but not what I said; I was too excited, I think. Anyway, after thinking about it for a while, I can finally put it into words—probably:

Our normal lives are pretty boring most of the time. My brother and I go to school every day; we work hard (I'm not sure my brother does); and we come back home and do the same thing the next day. Going on an adventure is a great way to break out of this routine. It helps us forget who we are and the problems we have—for a little while, at least. An adventure can be anything; it doesn't mean you have to climb Mount Everest. It could be walking in a park you've never been to before or trying some new type of food. You have to experience something new. You've heard this before, but we only live once. That's why a little risk is worth it. When you get out of your routine and go beyond the limits of your comfort zone, like I did when I went to the adventure camp, you're learning to take care of yourself and to grow. And, like when we helped Molly on our expedition, you're also learning to take care of those around you, and those around you are doing the same—adventure brings out the best in people, I think.

Goodbye, Lake District!

OK, time to go! Mom and Dad are here. I hope you've enjoyed my blog posts!

Key Words

1 Complete the sentences with a word or phrase from each box.

> comfort　go beyond　intense　first-aid　sprain

> your limits　rush　your wrist　zone　experience

a Are you OK? We should take you to the doctor to make sure you didn't
_____.

b If you want to be the best, you'll need to push yourself and
_____. Go on, you can do it!

c He doesn't want to go to an adventure camp. He likes staying in his
_____ at home.

d I can bandage your leg. I have _____ and a kit with
all the supplies I need.

e I wasn't terrified, but I felt an _____ of adrenaline
when we went over the rapids in the raft.

Comprehension

2 Read the blog again and number the events in order.

a The adventurers did some basic first-aid training. ☐

b Kacey had an adrenaline rush while rappelling. ☐

c Molly sprained her ankle. ☐

d Kacey's parents told her she was going to an adventure camp. ☐

e Jed and Emma told the group they have done well. ☐

f Kacey climbed up the rock face. ☐

g The other participants are surprised Kacey can read a map. ☐

h The adventurers find the campsite after hiking in the rain. ☐

3 Read and circle *T* (true), *F* (false), or *DS* (doesn't say).

a Kacey has never liked being adventurous. T F DS

b Kate and Russel both wanted to be at the camp. T F DS

c On June 13, Kacey spent most of the day thinking about
what was happening on her favorite show. T F DS

d Kacey didn't like marshmallows before going to the camp. T F DS

e Molly hurt her ankle while they were rafting. T F DS

f At the end, Kacey thinks adventure camp is a great way
to improve yourself. T F DS

Digging Deeper

4 📖 Mark (✔) the reasons why Kacey uses the first-person point of view.

a To talk about her thoughts and feelings at different moments. ☐

b To persuade readers to agree with her opinions. ☐

c To give her opinions about different situations. ☐

d To give instructions for surviving in the wilderness. ☐

e To make the readers feel like she is talking directly to them. ☐

f To show her readers how her opinions change. ☐

5 Write notes in the graphic organizer.

Cause	Effect
a Kacey has been stuck in her room for two months.	
b She went rappelling.	
c Her mom and dad taught her how to read a real map.	
d She left her comfort zone at camp.	

Personalization

6 Imagine you are going to an adventure camp. Complete the schedule with activities you would like to do each day.

Adventure Camp

Monday	Tuesday	Wednesday	Thursday	Friday

7 Describe how the camp would make you feel.

_____

_____

3 How can we understand a work of art?

Key Words

1 🎧 **Preview the Key Words.**
3.1

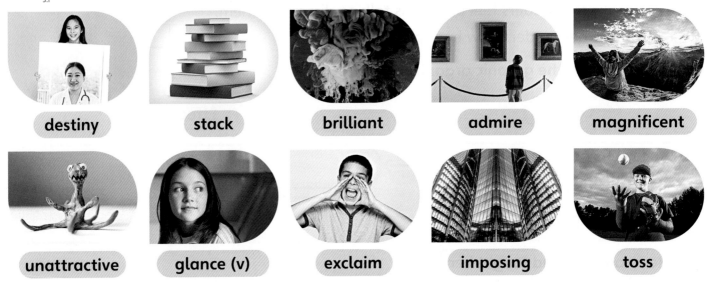

destiny   stack   brilliant   admire   magnificent

unattractive   glance (v)   exclaim   imposing   toss

2 Circle the word that doesn't belong according to its meaning.

a shiny, dark, brilliant, bright
b dislike, admire, appreciate, respect
c amazing, awesome, ordinary, magnificent
d throw, toss, hold, pitch

e unpleasant, ugly, unattractive, appealing
f imposing, small, awesome, huge
g goal, destiny, future, origin
h shout, exclaim, whisper, yell

Pre-reading

3 Look at the pictures on pages 33–37 and make predictions about the characters, setting, and theme.

a How old is the main character? What does she do?

_____

b Where does the story take place?

_____

c When does the story take place?

_____

d What is the topic of the story?

_____

4 🎧 **Listen and read.**
3.2

Rembrandt's Apprentice

By Kate Fitzgerald

Illustrated by Marco Antonio Reyes

Not everyone is lucky enough to know their destiny, but I am. I am going to be an artist. My desk is covered with jars of oil paint; brushes fill every corner of my room; and stacks of canvases remind me of all the images that I've painted. I've practiced for many hours in this room. And I've spent many additional hours observing the world around me. This summer, I've been working for Hendrick van Uylenburgh, the most famous art dealer in Amsterdam, and tomorrow he will have a very special guest—Rembrandt van Rijn. And I plan to meet him.

"It's getting late," says Mama when she comes into my room and finds me still at work. She places a fresh candle on my desk and winks at me. My sister comes in behind her and removes the old candle from my desk. She frowns at me, as she often does. She can't understand why I don't just want to find a nice Dutchman to marry. Mama and Papa understand my dreams. But my sister only shrugged the night Papa proudly hung one of my landscape paintings in our hallway.

It's early when I leave, and, as I reach the front door, I see my sister reading a letter. The morning light reflects off her hair. I notice her brilliant blue smock, and her mouth is slightly open as she reads. I wonder whether if it's a letter from her husband, who is away at sea. These are the kinds of moments that show the beauty of everyday life.

Outside the air is warm. Between the thick white clouds, I gaze at the bright blue sky. I hear water rush across rocks in the creek. The landscape is flat and green with wild trees stretching up to the sky. I stop and admire the quiet countryside before I enter into the busy city.

Men are stacking bags of tulip bulbs, fish, and spices along the docks. I'm always surprised at how the smell surprises me, even though I walk this way to work each morning. When I arrive at Mr. Uylenburgh's house, I see a magnificent sight: a large table covered in a thick cloth and baskets of fresh grapes and peaches. A half-peeled orange sits on the corner of the table; its peel forms a spiral. Wheels of cheese are stacked up high, and a lobster with an enormous claw sits near the edge of the table. However, I barely stop to look because I am so anxious to meet our guest. I scan the room to make sure I haven't missed Rembrandt's arrival.

Mr. Uylenburgh comes through the door and shouts, "Welcome to my home!"

His laugh is so loud that it scares me a little. A short man comes in behind him. Although his nose is large, it is not unattractive. In particular, I notice his confident smile, sparkling eyes, and nice clothes.

He begins, "Good Afternoon, I am—"

"Rembrandt van Rijn! It's an honor." The words come out of my mouth before I realize I'm speaking. I put my hands over my mouth as Mr. Uylenburgh looks at me a little disapprovingly.

Rembrandt smiles. "I see that you already know me."

"I admire your work enormously. I love how you leave the ugliness in your subjects' faces on display rather than painting perfect teeth or a beautiful nose. What fascinates me is your use of light in your portraits; it's something I haven't seen in anyone else's paintings. It's just spectacular!"

I glance toward Mr. Uylenburgh, who whispers, "Please excuse her … enthusiasm."

I was certainly talking a lot, but I didn't know if I'd have the chance to ever talk to Rembrandt again.

"I was enjoying what she said!" exclaims Rembrandt. "I prefer being with young people, and I admit that I like being complimented. And what is your name, young lady?"

"Geertryd!" I reply.

"Geertryd," smiles Rembrandt, "please accept an invitation to my studio. I'd like to know your opinion of my latest portraits."

I nod enthusiastically. To be invited to Rembrandt's studio is an incredible opportunity. I silently congratulate myself for speaking to him like I did.

"So, will you accept my invitation?" chuckles Rembrandt.

Just then, a man dressed in blue starts playing the lute.

"Of course I will!" I say, maybe too loudly, but I want Rembrandt to hear me over the music.

Rembrandt's studio is simple but has amazing light. An arrangement of a skull and flowers sits on top of an imposing table covered with a black cloth. "Memento mori," I whisper, remembering last night, when Rembrandt described this modern genre of painting to me.

He said, "It has no story—it shows the beauty of life and death, at the same time." And it's true; the contrast of the white skull against the vibrant flowers makes it so clear that life and death are always in the world together. It's a whole new way of looking at still life. I feel like I'm learning so much already.

Rembrandt doesn't seem to be aware of my presence. He mixes paints on a palette, using several brushes. He's painting a man with an expressive frown. Glancing at a small mirror on the windowsill, he sees me in the reflection and grins.

"There is no better model than yourself!" I grab my notebook and write as fast as I can. He laughs and says, "You are so enthusiastic! Today is about observing. I'm a careful observer of human nature."

He points to a blank canvas, and I approach. "Paint what you see—what you feel."

My hand shakes as I pick up the brush. But, then, I paint. I paint myself, but not as I really am. Instead, I'm a young woman in a formal black dress. I paint lace gloves and pearl earrings. As evening begins, Rembrandt leaves for another dinner, but he offers his studio for me to work in. I barely hear him leave as I finish the background of my self-portrait. It's not until I notice the morning sunlight that I realize I've worked through the night. I yawn and look for somewhere to rest. I have one of the maids send a letter to my mother, letting her know I am safe before lying down to sleep on the floor.

I wake up frightened and with a sore neck. The sound of keys in the lock tells me that there's no time. I hide underneath the table as the door opens. It's Mr. Uylenburgh and Rembrandt.

"Rembrandt! You have created another masterpiece!" Mr. Uylenburgh steps closer to my portrait.

"It is beautiful. I'm very fond of this work."

I'm overjoyed. Rembrandt is complimenting my work!

"I must have it!" Mr. Uylenburgh tosses a bag full of gold coins to Rembrandt. "Send it to my home, and don't forget to sign it!" he calls as he leaves.

Then—silence. Rembrandt approaches. The tablecloth is pulled back.

"You can come out now," says Rembrandt. I stand, embarrassed and brushing dust from my dress. Then, he sits down at his desk. I stare at my feet as he writes. After a long time, he hands me the piece of paper.

I can't believe my eyes. It's a contract for an apprenticeship. I will clean brushes, stretch canvases, and set up easels for money. But, I will also learn the art of portraiture from the greatest: Rembrandt van Rijn.

Key Words

1 **Read the opinions and match them to the pictures.**

a I think the **stack** of circles in this painting makes it seem like you're falling down a deep hole.

b This abstract painting is beautiful. I really like how the **brilliant** yellows contrast with the black.

c I'm not sure about Jackson Pollock's paintings. It looks like he just **tosses** the paint anywhere.

d *Self-Portrait with Velvet Beret* is my favorite Rembrandt painting. I like the way he is **glancing** back at the viewer.

Comprehension

2 **Circle the correct options.**

1 Who doesn't understand that Geertryd thinks it's her destiny to become an artist?

    a her mom   b her dad   c her sister

2 What does Geertryd like most about Rembrandt's work?

    a His paintings are realistic.
    b The way he paints teeth.
    c The subjects are attractive.

3 Who or what is Rembrandt painting when Geertryd arrives at his studio?

    a the table with a skull and flowers
    b himself
    c a woman in a black gown

4 How does Rembrandt pay Geertryd for the painting of hers that he sells to Mr. Uylenburgh?

    a He compliments her.
    b He gives her money in a leather purse.
    c He makes her his apprentice.

3 **Write the names of the characters from the story who would most likely say these sentences.**

> Rembrandt   Geertryd   Geertryd's mom   Geertryd's sister

a Why are you so interested in painting when you could get married?

_____

b I always paint self-portraits because it's cheaper than getting models!

_____

c I'm so excited to be able to learn from the best!

_____

d If you want to be a painter, go for it. Follow your dreams!

_____

Digging Deeper

4 **Complete the summary of the story with two sentences.**

Geertryd wants to be an artist. She meets Rembrandt at a feast at Mr. Uylenburgh's house. Rembrandt invites her to his studio. When she arrives, Rembrandt invites her to do a painting. Then, he goes out. Geertryd paints all night until she hears Rembrandt return. She hides under the table as Rembrandt enters the room with Mr. Uylenburgh.

_____

_____

_____

_____

5 **Circle the adjectives that describe Geertryd's personality.**

confident   lazy   artistic   angry   hard-working   unkind

6 📖 **What clues did you use to guess Geertryd's personality? Read and complete the character analysis chart.**

	Example from the Text	What You Can Guess
Her Words		Geertryd is _____.
Her Thoughts		Geertryd is _____.
Her Actions		Geertryd is _____.

Personalization

7 **Draw a self-portrait and write a short description. Choose any style (e.g., abstract, cubist, or modern)!**

_____

_____

_____

_____

_____

_____

3 How can we understand a work of art?

Key Words

1 🎧 **Preview the Key Words.**
3.3

surround   pause (v)   rewarding   appreciate   etiquette

distraction   scale   subtle   convey   mane

2 **Read the clues and write the Key Words.**

a If you find an experience really satisfying, you can call it this. _____

b Your phone rings while you're watching a movie. What do you press? _____

c Saying "please" and "thank you" are examples of this. _____

d A horse or a lion has one on its head and neck. _____

e When someone or something communicates information. _____

f The Internet can be one of these when you're trying to do homework. _____

g If there are things all around you, they do this to you. _____

h When something is not loud, noticeable, or obvious, it's this. _____

Pre-reading

3 **Look at the title of the blog on page 41. Write three reasons why you think you should see art in person.**

a _____

b _____

c _____

4 🎧 **Listen and read. As you read, underline important information and circle any words**
3.4 **or phrases you don't understand.**

Why Should You See Art in Person?

Imagine this: you're at the movies. The smell of popcorn is in the air; you take your seat in the theater; and the lights go down. The background noise disappears, and you switch off your phone. The music and sound effects surround you. As you focus your eyes on the giant screen, you enter into another world, undisturbed for the next 90 minutes.

Compare that experience to watching the very same movie in your living room. It's quite possible that you have popcorn, but you might have paused the movie in the middle to make it. You probably didn't switch off your phone. And you might talk during the movie with your family or friends who are sitting on the couch next to you. Is this experience the same as seeing the movie in the theater? It will not have the same impact, and you might find it harder to become engaged in the story.

It's similar when you look at art, like paintings, sculptures, or architecture. Seeing it in person can be a more rewarding experience than just viewing it in books or online. Like movie theaters, museums offer spaces dedicated to viewing and appreciating art. Museums require visitors to follow a kind of etiquette. For example, you will be asked to leave large bags at the visitors' desk, not only to protect the artwork but also so that you don't disturb the other visitors. For similar reasons, some museums don't allow flash photography. Once you enter a museum, your attention should be only on the art. Turn off the ringer on your phone, and try to focus on the art.

It's hard to focus when you're browsing the web or flicking through a book—there are so many distractions. We can be listening to music, talking with our friends, or texting while we're browsing images on a screen or on a page. In addition, books and websites don't allow you to appreciate the scale of a large piece of art or to see the details up close. Look at Claude Monet's *Haystacks* series. In a museum, you can view the tiny brushstrokes that make up the objects as well as their subtle differences of color. These are things that cannot be translated on a screen and that might change from one computer to another. And the images in a book are too small for the viewer to fully appreciate the detail or the size of some paintings.

Haystacks: **End of Summer**   *Haystacks*: **Snow Effect**   *Haystacks*: **Midday**

And what about a series or collection? You have to scroll, turn, or click from one page to the next to view art online or in books. You just can't experience the impact of a series of paintings if you don't see it in person. Imagine standing in the Musée de l'Orangerie in front of Monet's giant *The Water Lilies* or moving through two whole rooms of them! In each of the museum's two oval galleries, there are four large paintings of Monet's water lily gardens surrounding you. When you stand in the middle of the galleries, you have a 360-degree view. It feels as though you are standing in the exact same spot where Monet stood when he painted them. And, the sunlight that enters the gallery from the ceiling allows the viewer to experience the paintings differently depending on the time of day that they are there.

The Water Lilies: Green Reflections

What about art that's not inside a museum, you ask? Well, you have the activity of everyday life going on around you, but you can still better appreciate the details and size of a work of art in person. Take the famous Trevi Fountain in Rome. Being in the presence of Nicola Salvi's sculpture completed in 1762 allows you to appreciate the giant scale of the masterpiece. The fountain, with its marble sculptures, stands 26 meters high and is approximately 50 meters wide. There's no book or computer big enough to convey how large that is. And you can't appreciate the detailed texture of the robes and horses' manes. You have to be there to hear the sound of the rushing water and to see the lighting of the sculptures and the hundreds of people tossing coins into the fountain.

Trevi Fountain

Detail of Trevi Fountain

Or consider a piece like Richard Serra's sculpture *Connector*. This piece is nearly 20 meters tall and weighs over 325,000 kilograms. It is made of five curved pieces of steel that balance on one another. The sensation of walking into the middle of this sculpture is both exhilarating and terrifying. You know that the panels will not fall, but your instincts tell you that you are in danger. And then you look up through the opening at the top. It's inspiring, but the way you feel when you are in that spot, surrounded by these enormous steel panels, cannot be experienced by simply looking at a photograph.

So, for all these reasons, consider going to see art in person. It will be an experience that you may find fascinating, awe-inspiring, or even a little frightening. But, one thing is for sure: it will be far more rewarding than looking at the same works online or in a photograph.

Connector

Inside *Connector*

Key Words

1 Complete the dialogue with the correct form of the Key Words.

> surround   appreciate   rewarding   scale   subtle

Jim: I went to a cool gallery last weekend. Look, I took this photo of my favorite picture.

Emma: It looks like a mess.

Jim: Well, you can't really (a) _____ the (b) _____ of the piece. It was huge; you had to stand back to see all of it at once! Plus, it was (c) _____ by all these other paintings in the same series.

Emma: But the colors are so (d) _____. I don't see anything. What is it supposed to be?

Jim: Emma! Use your imagination. You can't see very well on the screen. In real life the colors were very bold. It was a very (e) _____ experience to see it in person. Maybe you just have to go to the gallery to see it for yourself.

Comprehension

2 Mark (✔) the reasons why we should see art in person according to the text. Check them against your ideas in Activity 3 on page 40.

a You focus your attention on the art. ☐

b It's similar to seeing it in your living room. ☐

c You find out more about the artist's life. ☐

d You get a better idea of size and detail. ☐

e You can get the artist's point of view. ☐

f You see the art where it was made. ☐

g You can research its history. ☐

h It inspires other feelings or senses. ☐

3 Write ideas from the text.

a Two distractions when you watch a movie at home:

_____

_____

b Two examples of museum etiquette:

_____

_____

_____

c Two sensations not possible from photographs:

_____

_____

Digging Deeper

4 📖 Read the first paragraph on page 43 again. Underline the information that refers to *who*, *what*, *where*, and *when* about the work of art. Then, complete the chart.

Who	Where
What	**When**

5 📖 Choose three of the words or phrases you circled as you read the text. Can you guess their meaning? Complete the chart.

I didn't understand:	Now I think they mean:	I guessed the meaning by:
_____ _____ _____	_____ _____ _____	• looking at the pictures. ☐ • reading the text again. ☐ • reading the words aloud. ☐ • using clues in the text. ☐

6 Write notes about two characteristics of each piece of art that people only appreciate in person.

Claude Monet's *Haystacks Series*	Monet's *The Water Lilies*
Nicola Salvi's Trevi Fountain	**Richard Serra's *Connector***

Personalization

7 Do you agree with the text? Complete the sentence with a reason of your own.

I agree / disagree that it is better to see art in person because _____

_____

How does information technology shape our lives?

Key Words

1 🎧 **Preview the Key Words.**
4.1

startle | virtual | labyrinth | disturb | blink (v)

solitary | gaze | wander | gasp (v) | thrust (v)

2 **Read the definitions and write the Key Words.**

a to interrupt what someone is doing, often by making noise _____

b to walk around without a clear destination _____

c to surprise or frighten _____

d to close then open your eyes quickly _____

e to breathe in suddenly and loudly with your mouth open _____

Pre-reading

3 **Look at the title and illustrations on pages 47–53 and answer the questions.**

a What do you think the title means?

_____

b Why do you think the illustrations have different styles?

_____

4 🎧 **Listen and read.**
4.2

REALITY LOST

BY ROBIN THOMPSON
ILLUSTRATED BY RICHARD ZELA

LEVEL: 237

SCORE: 2,600

237 LEVEL UP!

"Congratulations, Jimmy! You reached Level 237." The woman's voice in Jimmy's headphones startled him, so he turned the volume down on his VR headset and then scanned the new landscape. This part of the virtual city looked completely different from anything he'd seen before in the game. The buildings were much taller and closer together, and the empty streets between them were narrower. Something wasn't right.

Despite the new surroundings, the goal of the game never changed. Travel from your virtual "home" through an endless city and find as many golden discs as you can, then try to find your way home again.

Jimmy wondered if the city would ever end, but he didn't worry too much about it. Then, he moved his controller to direct his avatar through the labyrinth of streets and skyscrapers in search of the little golden discs that lay in dark, shadowy corners around the city.

A voice in the distance disturbed Jimmy. "Jimmy!" His mom's voice sounded strangely unreal after having spent so long in the virtual world.

"Coming!" shouted Jimmy. He waited until the numbers on his screen updated with his new score and then threw his headset aside, blinking from the sunlight. He felt dizzy as he stood up, but only for a few seconds. Then, he opened his bedroom door and ran downstairs.

His mom and his older brother, Luke, were already sitting in front of plates of roast beef, mashed potatoes, and gravy.

"Still playing that ridiculous VR game?" asked Luke.

"Level 237," Jimmy replied, ignoring his brother's tone. "I'm going to be school champion before long!"

"Oh," said his mother, "I didn't realize it was a school thing."

"It's not," said Luke, "but I bet everyone there plays it all the time. So, it might as well be."

Jimmy started to explain, "It's an online game, so, even though you play it on your own, you pass other players in the city who are also online and you can interact with them and everything! Although, most people don't—they're too busy looking for the discs."

"Well, that's not very sociable," said his mother with a frown. "Don't you play it, Luke?"

"There's no point. Nothing happens; there's no variety. You just collect these little discs, and that's it. It's a pointless solitary activity. I'd rather be outside doing something with my friends."

"You wouldn't think that if you played it, Luke," argued Jimmy. "It's fun discovering the new environments in each level, especially when you find the prizes."

"It's addictive, you mean," said Luke.

After dinner, Jimmy jumped up to leave the table, rushing back upstairs before his mom could shout, "Do your homework!"

When Jimmy put his VR headset back on, his avatar was looking down at the ground, motionless. "Oops! I forgot to log out properly."

He touched the controller, and his avatar jumped out of resting mode. He could see the virtual city again in his headset's built-in screen. As he moved farther down the street, he saw two more players who had obviously not logged out correctly either. Their avatars stood still, their heads down, like they were asleep. Jimmy recognized Adam, a boy in his class at school.

He thought the avatars looked creepy, their eyes open but staring down at nothing. He shivered. Even though it was just a game, he didn't like the feeling of being alone in this strange abandoned city—and the avatars, silent and still, added to his discomfort.

Suddenly, he heard footsteps behind him—not real footsteps, but the footsteps of another player. He jumped and turned his head toward the approaching figure. Jimmy recognized his friend Frank at once, and he felt a sense of relief. He turned his volume up.

"Hey, Jimmy, how do you like Level 237?"

Jimmy looked over at the frozen Adam. "I'm not a fan of it so far."

Frank's avatar followed Jimmy's gaze. "It looks like he forgot to log out."

"He's the fourth player I've seen like that today. It's weird that he's so close to that girl back there, too. You'd think he'd remember to log out after passing her," said Frank, waving behind him to a solitary avatar half a block away in the same state. Jimmy thought that he recognized her.

"Anyway, good luck." Frank's avatar walked past Jimmy in search of more golden discs.

LEVEL: 237

SCORE: 2,601

Jimmy suddenly ran after him. "Wait up, Frank!" Frank's avatar turned around.

"Why don't we look for some discs together?" said Jimmy hopefully. "Half and half on the points."

Frank looked thoughtful for a second and then smiled. "OK, why not? Better to get lost together, and you look pretty nervous for some reason, Jimmy." Frank laughed, but it was an unsure laugh that made Jimmy feel his friend would also be happy to have some company.

The two friends searched the virtual city for virtual kilometers in search of virtual golden discs. They hardly spoke to each other, but Jimmy was happy to have Frank by his side as they wandered deeper into the city. It seemed creepier the farther they traveled. Strangely, they hadn't found a single golden disc since they began their journey together. Even stranger was how empty the streets were. They saw no other avatars, either active or resting. It was as though they'd wandered into a completely undiscovered section.

Then, suddenly, Jimmy gasped. "Look!" He pointed. "Can you see it?" Just a few blocks ahead, a bright golden light in the blue surroundings.

"Finally!" said Frank. "Come on."

The two avatars jogged toward the light. When they reached the corner, the glow was so bright that it seemed to light up the whole city. Jimmy and Frank were about to be a whole lot richer—virtually, at least. They turned the corner and Jimmy nearly dropped his controller.

Six more avatars stood in the middle of the road, each with its head down, and each motionless; they all had the same lost expression that Jimmy had seen on Adam's and the girl's faces.

"Wow!" gasped Frank, who was staring at the piles of golden discs. "There must be at least a hundred discs here! Maybe more!"

Jimmy was focused on the frozen players; he'd never seen so many avatars together at one time in the game. He recognized one—a girl from school.

"Don't you think it's weird that six players all went offline at the same time, without actually signing out correctly, when there are so many discs here?" asked Jimmy.

Frank's excitement disappeared. He turned to face Jimmy, then slowly looked all around, as if something might be lurking in the shadows waiting to turn them into statues like the other players.

"What are you looking for?" asked Jimmy.

"I don't know," replied Frank. "But you're right—something's wrong here." Even as an avatar, it seemed as if Frank was concerned. Jimmy decided he'd played long enough for one night, so he accepted the pile of discs that Frank's avatar thrust into his virtual hands and said goodnight. He took off his headset, logged out, and started the homework he should have finished hours before.

51

The next day at school, Jimmy was tired. He hadn't slept well. He woke up several times from bad dreams that seemed so real they made his virtual-reality game look like an old-fashioned video game with bad graphics.

He became more worried even before the teacher finished taking attendance—Adam was missing. So during the morning break, Jimmy and Frank decided to go in search of the girl they had seen in the golden alley—perhaps she was missing, too.

"I haven't seen Rachel today," her friend said.

"What are we going to do?" asked Frank.

"I don't know," said Jimmy, "but I have a really bad feeling about this. It must have something to do with the game."

Jimmy found it difficult to focus on his schoolwork for the rest of the morning because he was too busy worrying about Adam and the other absent students. Then, before Jimmy could suggest to Frank that they sneak out of school to see if Adam was at home, there he was, sitting on a wall in the schoolyard, holding a VR headset in his hands, and talking to a blond girl. Suddenly, Rachel appeared and joined them.

"Look, Jimmy," said Frank. "It's the girl from the game!"

Jimmy walked over to them, pulling Frank after him. "Adam, what happened?" he asked. Adam looked terrible and serious.

The blond girl spoke for him. "Something happened to us all when we were playing the game last night. I guess I played for too long without taking a break. I suddenly felt dizzy, like when you first take off the headset, but this time, I was still wearing it. My eyesight became blurred, and then I fainted. I can't remember anything after that, until I woke up and was staring at the ground in the virtual city. I felt sick and had to get some fresh air, but I couldn't move. It really scared me."

"It happened to all of us the same way," confirmed Rachel. "I found a street full of golden discs, but before I could bend down to pick up even one of them, I felt dizzy and just froze."

"The game has started to affect all of us," said Adam finally. "Too much time in the virtual world. We need to warn others how dangerous it is."

Everyone agreed, so they started to talk to the people at school who they knew were playing the game. Some hadn't played for long enough to understand, but others had already experienced the same sensation. The group of students grew quickly, and the newer ones helped spread the message about the dangers of playing too much.

Jimmy came up with a name for the condition: *VBO (Virtual Burn-Out)*. He drew a logo, in the same style as that on the golden discs, so that people would easily recognize it. He made posters and put them up around the school. More students shared their experiences to help warn others.

One night, as Jimmy was tossing his VR headset into the garbage can, he thought about his new group of friends at school and how positive his life felt now. He realized he'd done more than escape the game—he'd beaten it. He'd found his way home, and it felt good to be back in the real world.

Key Words

❶ Replace each set of words in bold with the correct form of a Key Word.

a This part of the **computer-generated** city looked completely different from anything he'd seen before in the game.

_____

b The buildings and streets in the virtual world were a **set of confusing passageways.**

_____

c Jimmy's brother thought the game was a boring and **lonely** activity.

_____

d Jimmy was trying to focus on the game, but he was **interrupted and distracted** by his mom's voice.

_____

e As Jimmy stared at Adam's frozen avatar, Frank followed Jimmy's **unmoving look.**

_____

f Frank's avatar **pushed** a pile of golden discs into the hands of Jimmy's avatar.

_____

Comprehension

❷ Circle the correct option to complete each sentence.

a When Jimmy stops playing the game, he comes back to the real world **immediately / after a few moments.**

b Luke doesn't like the game because he thinks it's **addictive / boring.**

c Jimmy feels **nervous / cold** when he sees the motionless avatars.

d Jimmy and Frank saw **lots of / no** other avatars when they started to explore together.

e Jimmy had **bad / nice** dreams after logging out of the game.

f Adam and other students missed class because they were **sick / sleepy.**

g Jimmy beat the game by **collecting all the discs / returning to the real world.**

❸ 👤 Read and label the excerpts _L_ (limited) or _AK_ (all-knowing) narrators.

a Frank looked thoughtful for a second and then smiled. "OK, why not? Better to get lost together, and you look pretty nervous for some reason, Jimmy." Frank laughed nervously; he was still a little unsure. That made Jimmy feel his friend would also be happy to have some company. _____

b Jimmy found it difficult to focus on his schoolwork for the rest of the morning because he was too busy worrying about Adam and the other absent students. Then, before Jimmy could suggest to Frank that they sneak out of school to see if Adam was at home, there he was, sitting on a wall in the schoolyard, holding a VR headset in his hands, and talking to a blond girl. _____

Digging Deeper

4 Write notes in the story map.

Title: _____   Author: _____

Characters	Setting
Main Events	**Problem**
	Resolution
	Main Theme

5 Answer the questions.

a When do Jimmy and Frank start to realize something is wrong with the game?

_____

b Jimmy invents a name for the condition. Why does he choose that name?

_____

c Why does Jimmy feel positive at the end of the story?

_____

Personalization

6 Complete the poster with a piece of advice about playing video games or spending too much time online.

4 How does information technology shape our lives?

Key Words

1 Preview the Key Words.

slang

fluent

artificial intelligence

streaming

navigation

tedious

alert (v)

diagnose

recall (v)

preference

2 Match the columns.

1	If you speak a language well, you are this.	a a doctor
2	Streaming services can provide these.	b remember
3	You can use a navigation app on this.	c easy
4	This person diagnoses illnesses.	d movies
5	They can be coded with artificial intelligence programs.	e a preference
6	"Ez" is computer chat slang for this word.	f computers
7	If you recall something, it means you do this.	g fluent
8	If you like one thing better than another, you have this.	h a smartphone

Pre-reading

3 Look at the pictures on pages 57–59 and write two ideas in each column.

Things Computers Can Do Better than Humans	Things Humans Can Do Better than Computers

4 Listen and read.

Will Robots Replace Humans?

By Steph Kilen

There are many science-fiction stories about robots or computers replacing humans and taking over the world. But, could it really happen?

In 1637, philosopher René Descartes imagined a machine that would do many of the things that humans do. He wondered what it was that made humans unique and different from machines. He concluded that it was humans' ability to think that made them different. But, as computers become more and more powerful, people have started to wonder: can computers learn to "think" the way humans do?

Computers Put to the Test

How can we know if a computer is actually thinking? One way is to use the Turing test. It was developed in 1950 by Alan Turing. Many consider Turing to be the grandfather of computing. In the test, the tester exchanges text messages with a computer and with another human. The tester has to try to figure out which is which. The idea of the test is to see if a computer can "think" like a human—or, at least, seem to.

What about you? Have you ever used an online app to translate some text? In a way, you're performing a Turing test when you do. The translation app can tell you what the words mean. However, translating apps often can't understand the overall sense of a text. And, most translation apps don't understand slang or jokes. Now, think of asking a speaker fluent in two languages to translate for you. The answer they give you will be in language that is more natural. Natural language is one of the biggest factors in telling the difference between a human and a computer. And, at least in this case, computers fail the Turing test.

René Descartes

AI Is Already Taking Over the World

So, most computers can't understand a joke, but they sure are good at math! Computers do everything from adding up the cost of groceries to getting people into space. They take in information and come up with a mathematical answer based on that information. But what about all the things computers do that require more than math? That's where artificial intelligence, or AI, comes in.

We count on AI every day to do tasks quickly and accurately. AI does things we used to think only humans could do. It can use logic, make decisions, recognize human speech, and more. Our smartphones, social media, streaming services, video games, and navigation systems all use AI.

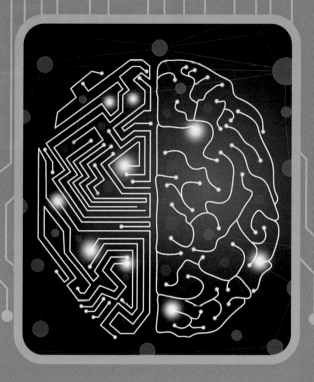

Navigation systems use AI technology.

Every job has tedious tasks, and AI can do a lot of those for us. That frees people up for more interesting and meaningful work. A famous experiment compared the abilities of lawyers and AI programs. Lawyers have to spend a lot of time going over legal documents. So, the testers wanted to see if AI would be better at this common task. It took the lawyers an average of 92 minutes to look through five documents. It took the AI program only 26 seconds! And the AI was 94% accurate, while the lawyers were right only 85% of the time.

AI makes the world more efficient, but it also makes it safer. When AI does a job, human workers are not put at risk. It can also get rid of human error that can cause dangerous problems. Some cars have AI systems that alert drivers to things they may not see so they can avoid accidents. Because AI is great at understanding and comparing data, it has also been helpful in diagnosing cancer and other diseases. So, AI might fail the Turing test, but it fails because it does these kinds of tasks so much better than humans can!

But Can AI Replace Humans?

The answer to that question may have to do not with *what* we think, but *how* we think. What we usually think of as "intelligence" has to do with recalling information and solving problems. These are things computers are definitely good at. But being human is about much more than doing tasks. It is about connecting with people and experiencing life with them.

You may not instantly know how to get anywhere in your city like a computer does, but you can certainly tell how people are feeling. And you are familiar with the variety of ways people show their emotions. In fact, you can feel sad when someone else is sad and want to make them feel better. This is emotional intelligence, recognizing and responding to emotions in all their different forms. Some people do it better than others, but we all do it better than computers. Therefore, computers may help doctors perform surgery, but they can't comfort patients who are scared about having that surgery.

The biggest drivers of our decisions are our preferences, or what we like or don't like. Because computers don't have emotions or our five senses, they don't have preferences either. The ways and reasons we develop these preferences make up our aesthetic intelligence. Some days you may like pineapple on your pizza, and some days you don't. And your friend may not want pineapple anywhere near her pizza.

What about our question: will computers replace humans? They might replace humans for some tasks, but not for all of them. So, go ahead and ask AI to find directions to the nearest pizza restaurant. But, if you want to be happy with your meal, it's probably best not to ask a computer to pick your pizza toppings.

Key Words

1 **Circle the correct options to complete the sentences.**

a Robots can do a lot of **tedious / interesting** and boring tasks in factories.

b This red light **diagnoses / alerts** you when there is danger ahead.

c Computers are good at information **navigation / recall**, but not so good at connecting with people.

d I'll make a decision based on my **preference / intelligence**—that is, which one I like better.

e Today, many people prefer to use **streaming / navigation** services at home instead of going to the movies.

f In order to **diagnose / alert** diseases, artificial intelligence has to interpret and compare data.

Comprehension

2 **Mark (✔) the things that computers or artificial intelligence can do better than humans. Compare them to your ideas in Activity 3 on page 56.**

a solve mathematical problems

b show emotions or comfort people

c look through legal documents

d think the way humans do

e make choices based on personal preferences

f understand and compare data

g understand the overall sense of a text that uses slang or jokes

h alert drivers so that they avoid accidents

3 **Answer the questions.**

a Why would a fluent speaker be more likely to pass the Turing test than a translation app?

b Why do AI programs that review legal documents fail the Turing test?

c What is emotional intelligence?

d How can AI make people safer?

e Why don't computers have aesthetic intelligence?

Digging Deeper

4 Write if artificial intelligence (*AI*) or humans (*H*) would be better at doing these things.

a giving a friend advice about what clothes to buy _____

b packing things in boxes all day long _____

c finding an address in a large city _____

d finding patterns in sets of numbers _____

e choosing a paint color for a room _____

f helping someone who is sad feel better _____

5 Complete each box with three ideas from the text and two ideas of your own.

(✔) Robots will replace humans.	(✘) Robots won't replace humans.
Ideas from the Text	Ideas from the Text
_____ _____ _____ _____	_____ _____ _____ _____
My Own Ideas	My Own Ideas
_____ _____ _____ _____	_____ _____ _____ _____

Personalization

6 🙂 Write your conclusion based on ideas from the text and your own ideas.

My Conclusion

I think robots _____ replace humans because _____

_____

_____

7 What are some ways that you use artificial intelligence regularly?

_____

_____

8 What is one thing you would like robots to do for you? Why?

_____

_____

How can we save the planet?

Key Words

1 🎧 **Preview the Key Words.**
5.1

rally   approve of   distrust   watch over   reusable

overreact   irritate   air quality   atmosphere   limp (v)

2 **Read the clues and write the Key Words.**

a If you suspect that someone is doing something wrong, then you do this to them.

_____

b This is all around us. It's the air we breathe. _____

c If you hurt your leg, you might walk like this. _____

d This is another word for "annoy" or "bother." _____

e This is an event where people get together to protest. _____

Pre-Reading

3 📖 **Look at the pictures on pages 63–67 and write predictions.**

a Setting: _____

b Characters: _____

c Plot: _____

4 📖 **Now write three things you want to find out when you're reading.**

First, I want to find out _____

Then, _____

Finally, _____

5 🎧 **Listen and read.**
5.2

All the Way into the City

By Sarah Steinberg • Illustrated by Emmanuel Urueta

The highway into the city was built without a pedestrian walkway because, when it was built, nobody thought people would ever want to walk if they didn't have to. And, not once in her life, had Sophia seen anyone walking it—well, except that one time. The guy was only sort of walking and mostly stopping to stick his thumb out—some guy with a backpack and wearing a baseball cap. Sticking your thumb out like that, her mom told her, meant he wanted a ride. It was an old-fashioned way of getting around called hitchhiking. Her mom didn't even slow down as they drove right past him.

"Why didn't you stop?" Sophia asked.

"I just don't want a stranger in the car with us, Sophia," her mom said.

Sophia thought about how sad that was. But now, she thought, as she walked along the side of the highway with cornfields on both sides of it, that would have to change. The climate crisis was getting too serious. People would have to share more, listen more, trust each other more. Wouldn't they?

When Sophia told her parents that she was going to walk all the way into the city to get to the climate rally, her mother offered to drive her. Sophia said no. Dad argued with her, but Sophia couldn't be persuaded.

"I'm going to a climate rally," she explained. "I'm going to get up there and give a speech about the small changes we can all make, even young people, to reduce our carbon footprint. I am not driving there!" Her parents could see the logic in that, but they didn't want her to walk by herself. It wasn't unsafe, exactly, but like the hitchhiker, it just wasn't how things were done anymore. It was decided that her older brother Oliver would go with her. Now he walked behind her, walking slowly and kicking at the gravel—like a character in a boring movie, thought Sophia.

Oliver didn't want to go. He didn't approve of his sister's activism. He distrusted it, in fact. Sophia was always doing things for attention, wasn't she? And now their parents were treating her like she was some kind of Greta Thunberg, so special and unique, and sending him out to watch over her as if he didn't have his own life. But he did have his own life! He kicked at the gravel. When he looked up, Sophia was standing a few feet in front of him.

"I packed a bottle of tea. Do you want some?" she asked him.

"Uh, sure," he said.

Sophia poured some tea into her reusable cups and passed one to Oliver.

"I can't believe it," Oliver said.

"What are you talking about?"

"Do you carry reusable cups everywhere you go? You must think you're so much better than everyone else."

"Oliver, have you been keeping up with the news at all? Did you know that global warming is a global crisis? Do you have any idea what the greenhouse effect is?"

"Don't overreact," he said.

Oliver didn't think there was a global crisis. If there was one, why wasn't it on the news? And if it was such a crisis, why weren't emergency sirens going all the time? And—this one really irritated him—if it was such a crisis, how could skipping school be the answer?

"Yeah, remind me when you're wearing a face mask outside," Sophia said.

They stood there in silence for a few minutes, watching the cars speed by along the road. Oliver had actually seen people walking around with surgical masks on their faces, but he had no idea why.

"What is that supposed to mean?" asked Oliver.

"Well, our air quality is getting worse all the time."

"What does that have to do with your reusable cups?"

He expected her to roll her eyes and say something to make him feel silly. But Sophia turned to him and said, "Pollution causes poor air quality. And air pollution is caused by the fossil fuels we burn to drive cars or fly airplanes. It creates gases that trap heat in the atmosphere."

"Sure, but what does that have to do with your cup, Sophia?"

"I'm getting there. So, as Earth's temperature rises, it creates all these other problems. The oceans' temperatures rise, and that creates all kinds of crazy weather. You've seen it on the news, right? Fires? Hurricanes? Extreme weather events, that's what they're called."

Now Oliver was getting impatient. "What about your cup?"

"I use this reusable cup because I'm trying to make small, everyday choices to help conserve energy and reduce the amount of waste that I produce. I can't vote, and I can't drive, so I'm focusing on what I actually can do."

To Oliver, that sounded somewhat reasonable. But it was still confusing. "I still don't see how walking to a rally is going to save the polar bears."

Sophia had nothing to say to that. As they started walking along the side of the highway again, sipping from their cups, they watched car after car drive by.

"You're right," Sophia said. "It probably won't save the polar bears. Maybe they'll go extinct."

A big truck drove by. As it did, the driver tossed a plastic bottle out of the window. It landed with a bounce on the other side of the highway. Sophia looked at her brother and raised an eyebrow. Oliver was taught not to litter. He would never throw something out of a truck like that. But, until now, it had never occurred to him that by not paying attention to things like driving or using plastics he was destroying his planet.

"I'm going to go get that," Sophia said, pointing at the bottle on the side of the road.

"You're going to cross the highway for a plastic bottle?" Oliver asked, like he couldn't believe what he was hearing.

"Yes," Sophia said.

"That's really stupid."

"Just hang on."

Sophia ran across the highway, picked the bottle up, checked to make sure there were no cars coming, and then ran back. But, as she did, Oliver saw her twist her ankle. She didn't fall, but he could see something had happened that was causing her a lot of pain. She limped the rest of the way back.

"OK, you're right. That might not have been the best idea," Sophia said.

"Now you think so?" Oliver asked.

"I think I sprained my ankle."

Sophia could feel it beginning to swell. It really hurt. The pain made her want to sit down and give up on the day. But she thought about how early she'd woken up, how nervous she'd been to give her speech in front of a crowd, and how much she'd wanted to change at least one person's mind.

"Well you're obviously not going to walk now," Oliver said, shaking his head. "I'll call Mom. She'll pick us up."

"Wait," Sophia said.

She put her arm on Oliver's shoulder and took a tiny hop toward the road.

"Are you serious?" Oliver asked. "You can't limp the whole way into the city."

"I am serious," Sophia said. "You don't have to stay with me. But I'm going to that rally. Let's hitchhike."

"No way! That's not safe. I'll use an app," Oliver said. "If we share a ride with other people going to the rally, it won't be as bad for the environment."

"OK," said Sophia.

Oliver wasn't going to tell her, but he was actually kind of impressed with his little sister. "You can practice your speech while we wait. I'm listening."

Key Words

1 Complete the sentences with the correct form of the Key Word pairs.

> irritate/reusable   air quality/atmosphere   rally/distrust
> approve of/watch over   limp/overreact

a It really _____ me that we left our _____ shopping bags at home.

b "Ow! I can't walk! Look, I'm _____!"

"Don't _____! You didn't break your leg!"

c The _____ _____ is poor today. There is lots of pollution in the _____.

d Everyone met for the _____ at the main government building.

They _____ the politicians' promises to take action on the climate crisis.

e My dad didn't _____ _____ me going to the rally on my

own. So he said he was coming to _____ _____ me!

2 Circle the correct option to complete each sentence.

1 People who stick their thumb out for a ride are …

  a truck drivers.   b hitchhikers.   c activists.

2 Sophia and Oliver drink tea from …

  a reusable cups.   b a bottle.   c disposable cups.

3 People wear surgical masks because …

  a of pollution.   b they want to skip school.   c it is hot.

4 Sophia uses a reusable cup to …

  a annoy her brother.   b save polar bears.   c reduce waste.

5 After Sophia sprains her ankle, Oliver uses a ridesharing app to …

  a call their mom.   b go home.   c get to the rally.

3 Read the problems and write the solutions.

Problem	Solution
a Sophia's parents don't want her to walk by herself.	
b Sophia can't vote or drive, but wants to make a difference.	
c A truck driver throws a plastic bottle out of his window.	

Digging Deeper

4 **Answer the questions.**

a Which activities from the story are bad for the environment?

_____

b Which activities from the story are good for the environment?

_____

5 📖 **Check your predictions from Activity 3 on page 62. Then, complete the summary.**

The story takes place on a (a) _____ . The main characters,

(b) _____ and (c) _____ , are brother and sister. They

are walking to a rally where (d) _____ is going to give a speech.

They are walking because (e) _____ .

(f) _____ explains why she cares for the environment, and sees a

(g) _____ throw a plastic bottle onto the highway. She goes to get it

and sprains her (h) _____ . (i) _____ decides to stay with her.

He uses an app so they can (j) _____ a ride to the rally.

6 📖 **Look at the purposes you set for reading in Activity 4 on page 62. What did you find out?**

a I found out _____

_____

b I didn't find out _____

_____

Personalization

7 **Do you think Sophia's decision to walk to the rally was smart or foolish? Explain why.**

_____

_____

8 **Complete the graphic organizer with activities you do that increase your carbon footprint or activities you can do to reduce your carbon footprint. Try to think of different examples than those in the text.**

Activities That Increase My Carbon Footprint	Activities That Can Reduce My Carbon Footprint
a _____	a _____
b _____	b _____
c _____	c _____

5 How can we save the planet?

Key Words

1 Preview the Key Words.
5.3

threaten

scarcity

substitute (v)

decrease

reliance

disposable

biodegradable

particle

trendy

distinctive

2 Match the Key Words to their opposites.

1 scarcity
2 decrease
3 reliance
4 threaten
5 trendy
6 distinctive

a independence
b old-fashioned
c abundance
d similar
e raise
f save

Pre-Reading

3 Look at the pictures on pages 72–78 and mark (✔) the three main topics discussed.

a deforestation ☐
b food ☐
c traffic and pollution ☐

d plastic ☐
e fashion and clothes ☐
f animals ☐

4  As you read the magazine article on pages 71–77, reread sentences or parts of the text you don't understand. Underline the sentences you reread.

5 🎧 Listen and read.
5.4

Take Steps to Reduce Your Carbon Footprint and Save the Planet

We often hear that our planet is under great stress from our ever-expanding carbon footprint, but what is a carbon footprint, and how can we reduce it? What are some ways we can help the planet?

Your carbon footprint is the amount of greenhouse gas that you produce from your everyday activities. Everything from riding in a car, getting the food you eat or the clothes you wear to the stores, or even heating and cooling your home contributes to your carbon footprint.

We need energy to do these activities, and most of this energy comes from burning fossil fuels, like coal or gas. By burning fuel, you produce a gas called carbon dioxide. Carbon dioxide and other gases like it are known as greenhouse gases. These end up in our atmosphere, and they cause the temperature of the Earth to rise. This is also known as global warming. If global warming continues, it will change the planet for the worse. For example, it might be hard for plants to grow. Animals will be affected because they will struggle to find food. They may have to migrate to find suitable habitats. If they can't, they might become extinct. And, places that are normally hot, like southern Europe, could become deserts. Other parts of the world might suffer from increased snowfall and rainfall. And, other regions will be threatened by wildfires, shortages of drinking water, and lost crops.

Natalie Dogan

Anne Williams

How can we reduce our carbon footprint?

There are lots of different ways we can reduce our carbon footprint: by turning off lights, turning off and unplugging our computers, recycling, reducing water usage, and walking and riding bikes instead of traveling by car. But there are so many more! Let's ask some experts about some other easy ways we can all help out.

Our teen correspondent for *Eco-News*, Natalie Dogan, has interviewed three different experts about what we can do to help save the planet. Let's listen.

Natalie: Hi, Anne! Can you tell me about your job?

Anne Williams: Good morning, Natalie! I'm a climate scientist, and I work on ways we can change what we eat to reduce our carbon footprint.

Natalie: Is my lunch today good for the planet? I have a baloney and tomato sandwich and some mango and strawberries.

Anne Williams: That sounds delicious, but it may not be the most eco-friendly! Let's take it step by step:

First, I recommend that you eat less meat. Livestock, such as cows and sheep, release large quantities of methane, a powerful greenhouse gas, into the environment. Raising livestock produces as much greenhouse gas as all cars, trucks, and automobiles combined! Livestock also consumes huge amounts of resources, like water. To get half a kilogram of beef, it takes around 20,000 liters of water. Think about how much water it took to make that baloney. Animal agriculture is the largest consumer of water in the world, and it could lead to water scarcity in many areas.

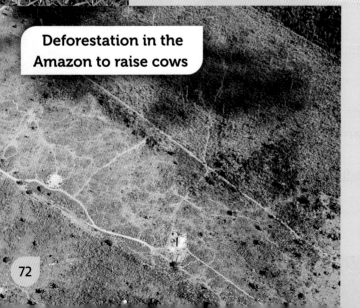

Deforestation in the Amazon to raise cows

You also have to take into consideration how the transportation and packaging of meat affects the environment. For example, transporting meat, especially long distances, requires large amounts of fossil fuels.

Instead of eating meat, you could choose a vegetarian diet, where you don't eat meat or fish, or a vegan diet, where you don't eat any animal products at all: no meat, fish, shellfish, dairy, eggs, or even honey. That will go a long way to reducing your carbon footprint.

Natalie: What can we eat then? It doesn't sound like a vegan diet leaves us with much to choose from!

Anne Williams: A vegan diet can be very tasty. It would include lots of different fruits, vegetables, nuts, grains, beans, and seeds. It is very beneficial for the planet! If we all became vegan, we would be able to reduce greenhouse gas emissions by 49%. Even substituting a weekly plant-based meal for a meat-based meal would make a huge difference!

A vegan diet

Buy locally-grown food

But it's not just about eating less or cutting out meat. Let's look at your mango and strawberries. Mangoes don't grow in this country, so your mango has traveled a long way to get to your store. We do grow strawberries, but not during the winter, so they traveled a long way to get to you, too.

The best thing is to buy and eat locally-grown or locally-produced foods that are in season. A person who eats this way is called a "locavore." It's winter now, and apples are grown in this region. Buy local apples instead of fruit that has traveled long distances. Buying locally produced, organic, and unprocessed foods from farmers is a great way to support your local community and economy, too!

You can also plant your own garden! You can grow all sorts of organic fruits and vegetables. It's great for the environment, since it helps to reduce your carbon footprint by decreasing the number of miles it takes to transport food from the farm to your plate. It also helps you to eliminate about one kilogram of carbon dioxide for every half kilogram of produce you grow. And it saves water, too. It's a great activity to do with friends and family. You can also plant trees, which help remove carbon from the atmosphere.

Natalie: Those are all great ideas! I think I can give up meat at least once a week. And I love apples! Thank you so much!

Plant your own garden!

73

Next, Natalie speaks to Professor Irving Johnson, a materials scientist who is researching how we can reduce our reliance on plastic.

Professor Johnson

Natalie: Hello, Professor Johnson! So, what advice can you give us to save the planet?

Professor Johnson: Hi, Natalie! Do you know much about plastic?

Natalie: Not really. Just that so many things are made of it!

Professor Johnson: That's right. A lot of the things we use every day are made of plastic. We don't recycle much of it, and that is a big problem for our planet.

Plastic waste in the ocean

Natalie: Can we burn it?

Professor Johnson: Unfortunately, plastic is burned, but it is very bad because it releases a lot of greenhouse gas into the atmosphere. Plastic is also filling up our oceans with terrible effects on our marine ecosystems.

Natalie: That sounds horrible! Can you give me some examples of plastics?

Professor Johnson: The worst kind of plastics are called single-use plastics, or plastic that is used only once and then thrown away, like most straws, cups, plastic bags, water bottles, and a lot of food packaging. Disposable plastic like this is made from oil. It's difficult to recycle and is not biodegradable.

Natalie: What does "biodegradable" mean?

Professor Johnson: Biodegradable products decompose into a natural substance, like soil. An apple takes about a month to decompose. Plastic, however, does not break down into a natural substance. Instead, it takes many—too many—years to break down into tiny particles. A plastic bottle can take 450 years to break down! In the process of breaking down, plastic releases toxic chemicals that then make their way into our food and water supply. These toxic chemicals are now being found in our own bodies, and they can be very harmful to our health.

Single-use plastic

Natalie: What can we do?

Professor Johnson: We need to use less plastic. So here are four things we can do:

First, we should stop buying plastic water bottles. Instead, use a glass or stainless steel bottle and refill it.

Next, we should bring our own cloth or canvas bags when we go shopping. In most countries now, you have to pay for plastic bags. In some places, plastic bags are outlawed. Bring your own bag or basket, and save some money and the environment!

Also, take your own containers to grocery stores and restaurants to reduce the disposable plastic packaging you take home.

And, finally, cook at home instead of getting take-out food. A lot of the take-out food we buy is packaged in single-use plastic. Cooking at home is tastier, healthier, and cheaper, and you have the added bonus of protecting the environment!

Natalie: That's great advice, but are there any eco-friendly alternatives to plastic?

Professor Johnson: There are plant-based plastics or bioplastics. Instead of being made out of oil, they are made from plants and are fully biodegradable. They are also less harmful to our health than normal plastics.

Natalie: So why don't we just replace all traditional plastics with bioplastics?

Professor Johnson: It's not that easy yet. Bioplastics are expensive to make, and not all of them are as strong as traditional plastics. But more and more research is being carried out to improve bioplastics and reduce their costs. Hopefully, with time, people will use more plastic alternatives. It just takes awhile.

Natalie: Thank you, Professor Johnson!

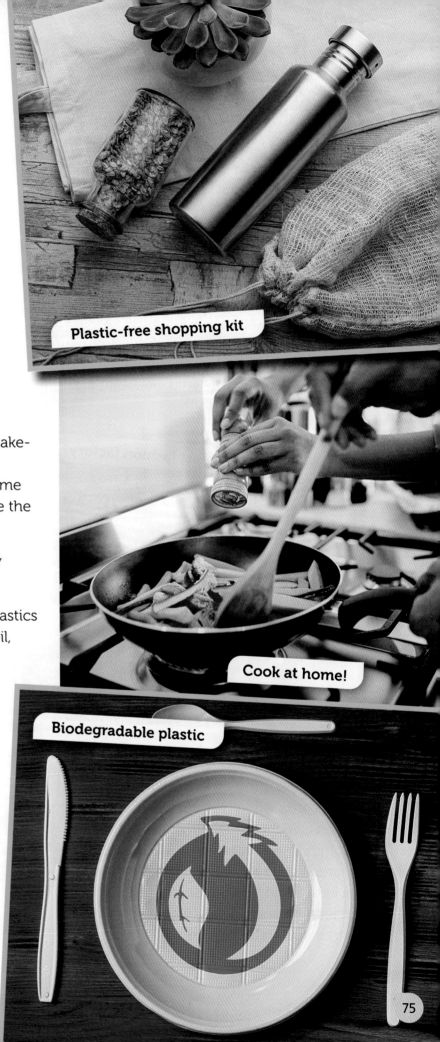

Plastic-free shopping kit

Cook at home!

Biodegradable plastic

Finally, Natalie speaks with Themba Adeleko—an expert on fashion and its impact on our global environment.

Natalie: Hi, Themba. What can you tell us about fashion and the environment?

Themba Adeleko: Hello, Natalie. Most people are unaware of the link between the fashion business and harm to the planet. The fashion business is one of the biggest polluters in the world. It is responsible for about 10% of the planet's carbon emissions, it dries up water sources, and it pollutes rivers and streams. People are buying more and more cheap, trendy clothes. This is called fast fashion. In fact, on average, people bought 60% more pieces of clothing in 2014 than they did just 14 years before. All of that means they are throwing away clothes more quickly, and these unwanted clothes are either burned or end up in landfills. Some experts estimate that a whole garbage truck full of clothing is dumped into a landfill every second!

Themba Adeleko

Fast fashion factory

Natalie: That's awful! What about what I'm wearing?

Themba Adeleko: It takes about 7,500 liters of water to produce the pair of jeans you're wearing. That's the same amount of water that a person would consume if they drank a bit more than eight cups of water a day for ten years!

Natalie: What are some things we can do to help?

Themba Adeleko: You can take old clothes to clothes banks where you can recycle them, or you can give them to thrift stores. Buying your clothes from thrift stores is also a fantastic way of creating your own distinctive style with unique items! And you can organize clothing exchanges with your friends, where you swap the clothes you no longer use.

Shopping at a thrift store

Themba Adeleko: Also, wash your clothes in cold water and dry them on a clothesline. It's better because you will not use energy to heat the water in the washing machine or use even more energy in a clothes dryer.

Moreover, try to buy clothes that are made out of natural fibers, like cotton and wool. Synthetic fibers are made from oil, and, when we wash them, they release tiny microfibers into the world's oceans and rivers. These microfibers often don't break down at all, and they are seriously harming the oceans' wildlife.

Clothes drying on a clothesline

Finally, stop buying the latest fashions. If you buy fewer clothes, you will reduce your carbon footprint in two ways. First, you won't be responsible for the environmental damage that occurs during the manufacturing of your clothes. And, second, you won't be responsible for the damage done when those clothes are transported from poorer countries in Asia to your local store. Plus, who wants to buy the latest fashions and look like everyone else? Develop your own style by swapping with your friends or shopping at thrift stores.

So, my top tips are: buy fewer clothes, take care of the clothes you do have, buy better-quality clothes that last longer instead of fast fashion, buy clothes made of natural fibers, and recycle.

Natalie: Thank you, Themba! I'm going to organize a recycling bank for clothes at school right away. And maybe some of my friends will be interested in a swap. It sounds like fun!

A clothing swap

We hope that you learned some new ways to take little steps that can have a big impact on the environment. We would like to thank Natalie and our three experts. We all need to work together to be more eco-friendly and reduce our carbon footprint. So, if you have more advice, please write to the editors of *Eco-News*. We would love to hear from you!

Key Words

1 **Use the correct form of the Key Words to complete the sentences.**

a Microfibers do not break down because they are not _____.

b Vegans can _____ rice and beans for meat in their diet.

c Environmental scientists are worried because _____ of plastic have been found in the oceans.

d _____ plastic cups are very bad because they can't be reused.

e I was surprised that producing _____ clothes can cause so much damage to the environment.

f Raising a lot of cows for beef can lead to a _____ of water.

Comprehension

2 **Mark (✔) the better option in each pair based on the text's advice.**

a Eat less meat. ☐   Raise more livestock, such as cows. ☐

b Find ways to buy exotic fruit from different countries. ☐   Become a locavore. ☐

c Grow your own garden. ☐   Buy organic fruits from other countries. ☐

d Make sure we throw plastic in the trash can. ☐   Use less plastic. ☐

e Refill and reuse containers. ☐   Buy bioplastic containers. ☐

f Cook at home. ☐   Eat in restaurants. ☐

g Take our old clothes to a landfill. ☐   Take our old clothes to a thrift store. ☐

h Use a washing machine and dryer. ☐   Wash clothes in cold water and dry them on a clothesline. ☐

i Buy fewer clothes. ☐   Always follow the latest fashions. ☐

3 **Complete the the sentences with words from the article.**

a G __ __ __ __ __ w __ __ __ __ __ __ is when the temperature of the Earth rises.

b Animal a __ __ __ __ __ __ __ __ __ __ __ consumes a lot of water.

c Trees help reduce the amount of c __ __ __ __ __ d __ __ __ __ __ __ in the atmosphere.

d B __ __ __ __ __ __ __ __ __ __ are plant-based plastics.

e S __ __ __ __ __ __ __ __ fibers are made from oil.

f Cotton and wool are examples of n __ __ __ __ __ __ fibers.

Digging Deeper

4 📖 Which sentences did you reread? What do you think these sentences mean now?
Write two examples in the graphic organizer.

Sentences I Reread	What I Think They Mean Now
a	a
b	b

5 📖 Reread what each person talks about and answer the questions.

Anne Williams

a Why is animal agriculture so damaging to the environment?

_____

b How does being a locavore reduce your carbon footprint?

_____

Professor Johnson

c How do single-use plastics damage the environment?

_____

d Why aren't plant-based plastics a solution yet?

_____

Themba Adeleko

e How is "fast fashion" harmful to the environment?

_____

f How do clothing swaps reduce your carbon footprint?

_____

Personalization

6 How useful are the tips for reducing your carbon footprint in the article? Do you do
any of these things already? Write notes in the graphic organizer.

Area	Things I Do Already	One More Thing I Can Do
Food		
Plastics		
Clothing		

6 What makes a good story?

Key Words

1 **Preview the Key Words.**
6.1

exterior

lobby

skyscraper

engrossed

flutter (v)

trapped

gust

interior

flight of stairs

stairwell

2 **Match the Key Words to the words and phrases with similar meanings.**

1 exterior	a fly irregularly in the air
2 engrossed	b a sudden burst of wind
3 flutter	c inside
4 trapped	d the space inside a building's main entrance
5 gust	e fascinated
6 interior	f stuck inside something
7 lobby	g outside

Pre-reading

3 **Look at pages 81–85 and answer the questions.**

a What type of text do you think this is?

_____

b Which characters have speaking parts?

_____

c Where and when does the story take place?

_____

4 **Listen and read.**
6.2

A Hairy Situation

By Steph Kilen • Illustrated by Tania Juárez

SCENE 1. EXTERIOR. CITY STREET. DAY.

Lola, a medical student, waits impatiently at a bus stop on a busy, downtown street. Behind her stand the lobby doors of a skyscraper. She's engrossed in an enormous textbook as horns honk and cars rush by.

NARRATOR

In the big city, everyone is on a mission: to work, to be successful, to be the first person to do the next amazing thing. Lola just wants to catch her bus and prepare for an important test on the organs of the body. Nevertheless, she, too, is on a mission.

A paper flutters over Lola's head and lands in her open book. It says: "Help me!" Way up in the skyscraper, a man leans out the window, gesturing wildly. She can hear him yelling, but not what he is saying. She shakes her head to tell him she can't hear him, and he disappears back into the building. A moment later he reappears, sending down what looks like a rope, but, when it gets to Lola, she realizes it is actually his beard! To it, he has attached another note: "I'm trapped on the 45th floor. It's a matter of life and death. Help!!"

A gust of wind hits Lola from behind; she turns around to see the bus pulling away.

NARRATOR

Heroes do walk among us. They might not have superpowers or high-tech suits, but they are motivated to help people. The same instinct that inspires Lola to want to be a doctor tells her that now she has to help this man. All she has to do is go in the building and tell the security guard.

SCENE 2. INTERIOR. LOBBY. DAY.

LOLA

Excuse me. There's a man trapped on the 45th floor. If you could just …

SECURITY GUARD

(not looking up from her graphic novel)
There's no 45th floor.

LOLA

(looks at the note to see 45th is underlined)
He sent me this note, and it definitely says 45.

SECURITY GUARD

(looking up, clearly annoyed)
There's no 45th floor.

The security guard returns to her graphic novel. The next bus arrives in 10 minutes. Determined, yet anxious, Lola gets on the elevator and pushes the button for the 45th floor. She is alone.

SCENE 3. INTERIOR. ELEVATOR. DAY.

LOLA

(muttering)

There's no 45th floor. Hmpf.

NARRATOR

Being a hero is not straightforward, friends. If it was, we wouldn't retell the stories of their great deeds over and over. Have you ever heard a fairy tale about someone who saves the day by sneezing or zipping up their coat? I don't think so.

At each floor more people get on: a salesman wearing a spinning bow tie, a family wearing matching polka-dot sweaters, and elderly triplets with turquoise hair. Lola is trapped at the back of the elevator. The light indicates the 44th floor.

LOLA

(loudly)

Forty-five is my floor!

No one seems to hear her, and she watches as the light turns from 44 to … 46! The doors open, but she can't get through.

LOLA

(checking her watch, whispering to herself)

Just breathe. Get off on the next floor, and walk down the stairs. I still have four minutes.

She waits for the doors to open again. However, much to her dismay, the elevator just keeps going up. When it gets to the top floor, everyone gets out. The little boy drops his stuffed dinosaur, and Lola picks it up. But, before she can hand it to him, he is out of the elevator and the doors have closed.

LOLA
(frantically pushing all the buttons)

ARRRGGGGHHHH!

NARRATOR

What's a hero to do? Accept defeat? Or take the opportunity to prove her courage?

The elevator doesn't stop until it gets to the lobby, where Lola gets out and glares at the security guard. She looks toward the bus stop. She has missed the bus again. Then, she reads the note again: "It's a matter of life and death."

SCENE 4. INTERIOR. LOBBY. DAY.

MAN IN COWBOY HAT
(sitting on a shoeshine stand, pointing)

The stairs are that way.

LOLA

My next bus arrives in 15 minutes. It's the last one of the day. I will never climb 45 flights of stairs fast enough.

MAN IN COWBOY HAT

You better set her up, Eddie.

LOLA

I don't have time for a shoeshine!

EDDIE
(nodding his head toward the other seat in the stand)

Get up there. Trust me.

NARRATOR

It's hard to know who to trust, but even heroes need help.

From his shoeshine kit, Eddie pulls two large, glowing springs and straps them to the bottom of Lola's shoes.

EDDIE

You can hop a flight at a time with these.

MAN IN COWBOY HAT
(handing Lola a key)

You'll need this, too.

SCENE 5. INTERIOR. STAIRWELL. DAY.

Lola bounds to the stairs and up 45 flights. When she opens the door, she finds a high-tech lab with screens, whiteboards with chemical equations, a powerful microscope, test tubes, and vials. The man with the beard stands in the middle of it all.

SCENE 6. INTERIOR. MAN WITH THE BEARD'S LABORATORY. DAY.

MAN WITH THE BEARD

Thank you! I've sent so many notes. I think everybody gave up when the security guard said there was no 45th floor.

LOLA

What is this place?

MAN WITH THE BEARD

It's my lab. I didn't want to be disturbed, so I fixed the elevator to skip this floor, told the security guard not to tell anyone about it, and stopped communicating with the exterior world. And, I had Mr. Grimm, the man in the cowboy hat, lock me in. But then, I realized I hadn't planned on how to tell him to let me out. I've been here a very long time. I don't know how long; I didn't have a beard when I got here. But I've done it! And now that you've rescued me, I can tell the world about my discovery!

LOLA

Done what?

Before the man with the beard can answer, Lola realizes the last bus arrives in just four minutes. She doesn't wait for an answer and runs out the door and down the stairs.

SCENE 7. INTERIOR. LOBBY. DAY.

LOLA
(unstrapping the springs and tossing them to Eddie as she runs toward the door)

Thank you! You're a hero!

NARRATOR
**A hero's life is not all bounding up flights of stairs and saving the day, friends.
No, some of it is boring, tedious work.**

SCENE 8. INTERIOR. LOLA'S APARTMENT. DAY.

Lola is in her small apartment at a desk. She's reading the same humongous textbook. She rubs her eyes and groans, and then goes to the kitchen to microwave a frozen dinner. She turns on a small TV on the counter. On the screen is the man with the beard.

NEWS REPORTER
We're here with Dr. Jeff Rapunzel, who has just made an amazing discovery.

MAN WITH THE BEARD
I have discovered how to regenerate organ tissue so that people will no longer need transplants and can just regrow their own organs!

LOLA
Well, I guess it was a matter of life and death!

There is a knock at the door. Lola wipes her mouth, answers it, and finds a man, smiling shyly.

MAN WITH THE BEARD
I wanted to thank you in person.

LOLA
I'm sorry. Do I know you?

MAN WITH THE BEARD
Maybe you don't recognize me. I shaved. You saved my life yesterday—and the lives of many others. How can I ever repay you?

LOLA
Well, I do have an exam on organs coming up. Maybe you could help me study?

Lola invites Dr. Rapunzel in and pours him a cup of tea.

NARRATOR
You, too, can be a hero, friends. You never know when your daily routine will turn into a heroic mission.

85

Key Words

1 Complete the crossword puzzle with Key Words.

Down

1 the space in a building where the stairs (for multiple floors) are

4 a sudden, quick rush of wind

Across

2 a _____ of stairs goes from one floor of a building to the next

3 a very tall building

5 to be so focused on something that you ignore everything else

6 a large area inside the entrance of a building

Comprehension

2 Complete the sentences with one or two words.

a Lola is waiting for a bus to go to _____.

b When she reads the _____ attached to the man's beard, she decides to help.

c The security guard says there is no _____.

d The elevator goes to the top of the skyscraper and back down to the _____.

e Eddie gives Lola some _____ to hop up the flights of stairs.

f The man has a long beard because he has been trapped in his _____ for a very long time.

3 Answer the questions.

a What does Dr. Rapunzel discover?

_____

b How does he repay Lola?

_____

c Why is the movie called *A Hairy Situation*?

_____

Digging Deeper

4 📖 Complete the Venn Diagram with words and ideas from the box.

characters   dialogue form   present tense   narrative (past) tenses
chapters   scenes   plot   setting   prose

Movie Script   Both   Story

5 Write about why each person from the script is a hero.

Lola: Why is she a hero? What did she do?

_____

_____

Dr. Rapunzel: Why is he a hero? What did he do?

_____

_____

Eddie: Why is he a hero? What did he do?

_____

_____

6 Does this movie script remind you of any fairy tale that you know? How?

_____

_____

Personalization

7 Read the quotation from the script and write about an everyday hero you know.

Heroes do walk among us. … They are motivated to help people.

Name of Hero: _____

Why is he or she a hero? _____

_____

_____

6 What makes a good story?

Key Words

1 🎧 **Preview the Key Words.**
6.3

cottage

porridge

troll

series

dire

illustration

property

obey

overcome

persuade

2 **Complete the sentences with the Key Words.**

a I had to _____ my fear of heights when I went rock climbing.

b We were hungry and lost in the forest. It was a _____ situation.

c He tried to _____ me to read the book, but I wasn't interested.

d Does your dog _____ you? Mine does! It sits when I tell it to.

e My little brother has no respect for other people's _____. Last week, he broke my cell phone and didn't say he was sorry.

f The pictures in this book are more frightening than the words. Look, this _____ is really scary!

g The family lived in a small _____ in the woods.

h There are a lot of folktales in which a _____ lives under a bridge.

Pre-reading

3 **Look at the title and pictures on page 89. Write one way each fairy tale might be scary.**

a "Hansel and Gretel" _____

b "Little Red Riding Hood" _____

c "Goldilocks and the Three Bears" _____

d "The Three Billy Goats Gruff" _____

4 🎧 **Listen and read.**
6.4

Scary Fairies:

Should Fairy Tales Be Frightening?

By Susannah Reed

Have you ever heard someone say "It's like a fairy tale" when something really good happens? So, fairy tales are set in a perfect world, where everyone is happy, right? Wrong! Read the blurbs to these famous fairy tales. How are they similar?

"Hansel and Gretel"

Hansel and Gretel's stepmother abandons them in the middle of a forest. Lost and hungry, the children find a cottage that is made out of candy. They start to eat the house, and a kind old woman comes out and invites them in. But the woman is really an old witch who wants to eat them! How will they escape?

"Little Red Riding Hood"

Little Red Riding Hood is going to visit her grandmother, who lives in the middle of a forest. On the way, Little Red stops and tells a friendly wolf where she is going. The wolf runs to the grandmother's house, eats her, and gets into her bed. He wants to eat Little Red, too. Who will win? Little Red or the wolf?

"Goldilocks and the Three Bears"

Goldilocks goes into a cottage in the middle of a forest. She finds three chairs, three bowls of porridge, and three beds. She sits on and breaks the smallest chair, eats the porridge in the smallest bowl, and falls asleep in the smallest bed. When the three bears return home, they are very angry. What will happen to Goldilocks?

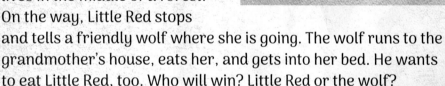

"The Three Billy Goats Gruff"

The Billy Goats Gruff want to eat the delicious grass in the fields on the other side of a bridge. There is just one problem. A troll lives under the bridge, and his favorite food is goat! How can they cross the bridge safely?

Did you notice that the main characters are in danger in all four stories? Why? A fairy tale shouldn't be frightening—or should it?

A Good Story Is an Exciting Story

A story is often more exciting if the heroes are in danger. We identify with them, and we are frightened for them. Therefore, we want to read to the end of the story and find out what happens. We want to know if they'll escape and how.

Why Is Danger Exciting?

Our bodies react to fear and excitement in a similar way. When we are excited, our bodies release a chemical called adrenaline. Our breathing and heartbeat get faster, and we sweat. When we are frightened, our bodies release the SAME chemical, adrenaline. So being a bit scared is exciting. Being scared can even feel good if you can predict it. When we read a scary story, watch a scary movie, or go on an amusement park ride, we may be afraid, but we also know we are going to be safe at the end of the experience. Therefore, our bodies release adrenaline, and our brain releases another chemical called dopamine at the same time. So feeling frightened also feels fun because dopamine makes us feel good!

Does Fear Make Fairy Tales Popular?

So, if being scared can be fun, is that why fairy tales are popular? It could be; people certainly like them. There are many different versions of "Little Red Riding Hood," and they come from all over the world. People have also been enjoying the story for a long time. Some versions of the story may be over 2,000 years old.

In some versions of the story, Little Red Riding Hood outwits the wolf.

How Is Fear Built into Fairy Tales?

Fear is built into fairy tales in different ways. One way is in the literary elements of the story: the setting, the characters, the plot, and the themes. Many fairy tales are set in a dark forest. People are often scared of the dark, and there is also the fear of the unknown. Fairy tale characters don't know what they will find in the forest. The villains are dangerous animals, such as wolves and bears, or scary fantasy characters, such as trolls.

A scary series of events in the story's plot also maintains the fear. In "Hansel and Gretel," for example, first the children are abandoned and get lost in the forest. Then, they are caught by an evil witch. Then, the witch makes Gretel into her servant and puts Hansel in a cage. Her final plan is to eat him!

The themes of the stories can be just as frightening as the fairy tale villains. Before they even meet the witch, Hansel and Gretel are in a dire situation. Their mother has died, and their new stepmother doesn't love them. Worse, she abandons them in the forest and leaves them all alone. The possibility of abandonment is very frightening to young children. Even when the children escape from the witch, the reader is still frightened for them. What will happen when they get home? Will they be safe with the stepmother now?

What Role Do the Illustrations Play?

Let's not forget the illustrations. Look at these two modern illustrations for "Hansel and Gretel." Then, compare them with the photograph above. What differences can you see? Which ones make the story look the scariest or least scary? Why?

So are fairy tales only frightening to make them exciting? No, they aren't! Many fairy tales aim to teach readers lessons about the world as well as themselves, and fear is used to help teach these lessons.

Lessons About the World

Many fairy tales show the difference between good and evil. In this way, the reader learns how to recognize danger around them. They also develop a sense of right and wrong as well as respect for other people and their property.

Most fairy tales have one or more morals, which are lessons the story wants the reader to learn. In "Little Red Riding Hood," for example, the morals of the story include obeying your parents and not talking to strangers. These are important lessons about keeping ourselves safe.

Bad things happen to Little Red Riding Hood because she doesn't listen to her mother's advice. She should have gone straight to her grandmother's house and not stopped along the way. She also learns that you can't trust strangers. She shouldn't have told the wolf where she was going. Although he seemed friendly, he planned to eat her!

Hansel and Gretel also learn not to trust strangers. The old woman seems kind, but she is really an old witch. Hansel and Gretel also learn they should respect the property of other people. They were hungry, but they shouldn't have eaten the witch's house!

Goldilocks has to learn to respect other people's property, too. The three bears should chase her out of their cottage—after all, they didn't invite her in. She went in when they were out, broke their furniture, and ate their breakfast!

Fairy tales also teach us lessons about how to deal with our feelings and how to solve problems.

Dealing with Our Feelings

Fear and other negative emotions are a fact of life, and scary stories help us learn to deal with them. When we read a scary story, we learn to overcome fear with the characters. It's good to learn to do so without personally experiencing the events in the story. In addition, if we understand what fear means, this makes us more understanding when other people are scared in real life.

Reading about scary events in stories also allows us to talk about them. Talking about things that frighten us is good. It helps us to tell the difference between real and imagined fears. We can also discuss ways of dealing with frightening events that do happen.

Learning to Solve Problems

Fairy tales can also show us how to solve problems, even when that problem is a hungry troll! The Three Billy Goats Gruff work together and use their cunning plan to outwit the troll. As each goat crosses the bridge, the troll appears and wants to eat him. Each time, the goat keeps calm and doesn't run away. Instead, he points to his bigger brother, who is coming behind him, and persuades the troll to wait for him. When the biggest goat arrives, the troll is tired and the big goat runs and pushes him off the bridge. The three goats can then cross the bridge and eat the delicious grass on the other side.

Should fairy tales be frightening? Of course they should! Readers have loved and learned from them for centuries. So, let's have more, not fewer, scary fairies!

Key Words

① Use the Key Words to solve the riddles.

a Don't let a problem make you quit.
You can do this, if you persist.

_____

b Lots of children are frightened of me;
I'm always a monster in stories, you see.

_____

c Do the words of the story help you see?
If not, then you can always look at me!

_____

d Eat me from a bowl and use a spoon.
But hurry up, the bears are coming soon!

_____

e I'm a group of events, one after the
other. When one event ends, along
comes another.

_____

f This is something that you own,
It could be land, a car, or a home.

_____

Comprehension

② Read and circle *T* (true) or *F* (false).

a Our bodies react in very different ways when we are excited or scared. T F

b Setting, characters, events, themes, and illustrations can add to the fear. T F

c Fairy tales can teach readers about good and bad behavior. T F

d Frightening themes from fairy tales have nothing to do with real life. T F

③ Think about how fear is built into each fairy tale. Check your ideas from Activity 3 on page 88. Where possible, write an example from each story in the chart.

	A Scary Setting	A Scary Character	A Scary Plot Event
"Hansel and Gretel"			
"Little Red Riding Hood"			
"Goldilocks and the Three Bears"			
"The Three Billy Goats Gruff"			

Digging Deeper

4 📖 **Mark (✔) the best description of the structure of "Scary Fairies."**

a   describes the order of events ☐

b   explains how two things are similar or different ☐

c   describes a problem and describes steps to take to solve it ☐

d   provides detailed information about a topic ☐

e   describes an event and the effects it has on something else ☐

5 📖 **What nonfiction text in this book has the same structure? A different structure?**

Same Structure: _____

Different Structure: _____

6 **Read each moral and write the name of the fairy tale that teaches it. There may be more than one correct answer.**

a   Stay calm and work together.

_____

b   Listen to the advice of others.

_____

c   Do not trust strangers.

_____

d   Respect other people's property.

_____

Personalization

7 **Do you agree with the article's conclusion? Why or why not?**

_____

_____

_____

8 **Write notes about a scary story you have read.**

Title: _____

Why was it scary? _____

_____

_____

What (moral) did you learn? _____

_____

7 Why do we need medicine?

Key Words

1 🎧 **Preview the Key Words.**
7.1

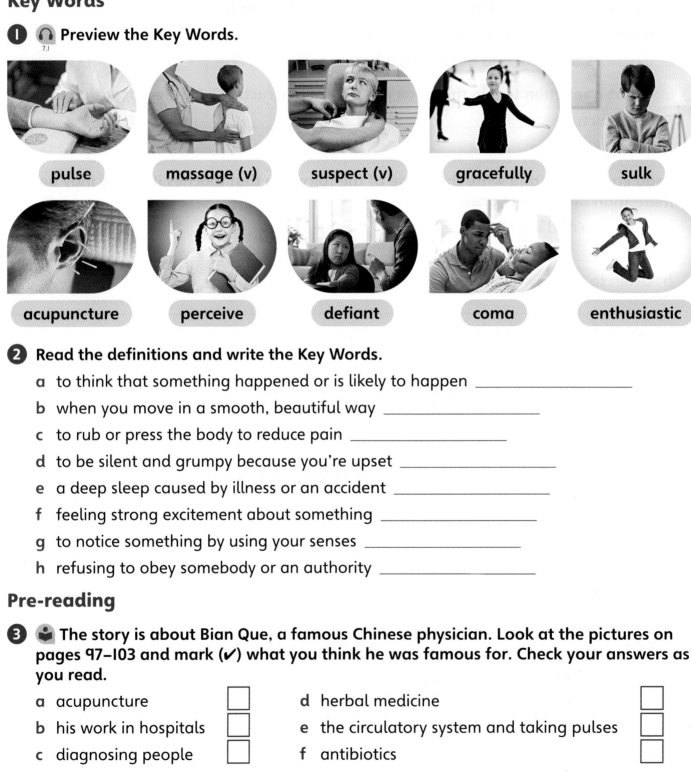

pulse   massage (v)   suspect (v)   gracefully   sulk

acupuncture   perceive   defiant   coma   enthusiastic

2 Read the definitions and write the Key Words.

a to think that something happened or is likely to happen _____

b when you move in a smooth, beautiful way _____

c to rub or press the body to reduce pain _____

d to be silent and grumpy because you're upset _____

e a deep sleep caused by illness or an accident _____

f feeling strong excitement about something _____

g to notice something by using your senses _____

h refusing to obey somebody or an authority _____

Pre-reading

3 📖 **The story is about Bian Que, a famous Chinese physician. Look at the pictures on pages 97–103 and mark (✔) what you think he was famous for. Check your answers as you read.**

a acupuncture ☐   d herbal medicine ☐

b his work in hospitals ☐   e the circulatory system and taking pulses ☐

c diagnosing people ☐   f antibiotics ☐

4 🎧 **Listen and read.**
7.2

The Racing Pulse

By Lucy Pawlak • Illustrated by Israel Ramírez

Linlin stands outside her son Nian's bedroom and says, "Knock-knock!"

"One second! Uh, I mean come in." When Linlin enters Nian's room, she finds him sitting at his desk. He turns to smile at her, looking as innocent as a baby. "Hello, Mom! What's up?"

"Hello, Nian. What are you doing?" asks Linlin, frowning.

"Well isn't it obvious?" The boy points sweetly at an open textbook. "I am working hard on my homework." Linlin looks around the room. The window is open, and a breeze blows in. Posters of dancers cover the walls. It looks like a space was cleared for some sort of activity that has suddenly stopped. The bed has been pushed against the wall, and the desk is sitting right next to it. Linlin looks at her son's red and sweaty face, and she notices he is rubbing his ankle. It doesn't seem to her like he was working, so she raises an eyebrow suspiciously.

"Oh, really? So, what exactly are you studying?" she asks.

"I'm learning all about the amazing history of Chinese medicine!" says Nian, a little hesitantly. Linlin can hear that Nian is out of breath; she can see that his ankle is causing him some pain, too; it looks a little swollen. "Why are you staring at me like that?" asks Nian.

"I just heard a lot of noise coming from up here and then a big crash, so I thought I should check if you're OK. Can I just …" She takes his wrist in her hand and measures his pulse; she frowns. "Are you sure you were working?"

"Yes," answers Nian, quickly pulling his wrist away and smiling nervously.

"Chinese medicine is a huge subject. What part are you studying?" she asks.

"The first doctor … from ages ago … His name rhymes with mine. Uh, it's … Bian …" Nian hesitates and glances at the pages of his book for the answer.

"I see," says his mother. "Do you mean Bian Que, the legendary Chinese physician who lived over 2500 years ago?" Nian nods slightly. "So, can you tell me about his four-step method?" she asks, looking hard at her son.

"No, I haven't gotten to that part yet," he replies, still massaging his ankle.

"Oh, that's funny because it's what Bian Que is most famous for. He used it to diagnose his patients. First, you have to look at their outer appearance. Then, you listen to their breathing. Next, you should ask how they feel. And finally, you take their pulse. For example, when I came in the room just now I looked at your outer appearance: red in the face and sweaty, even though the windows were open. I listened to your breathing and heard that you were also out of breath. And you have obviously hurt your ankle. Plus, I took your pulse, which was very fast. From all that, I diagnosed that you had not been working; instead, you were probably dancing."

"Just a little bit," protests Nian.

Linlin continues, "Actually, I already suspected that because the noise you made jumping around was coming through the ceiling. I guess you fell and sprained your ankle, which is why I heard a big crash."

"Mom, I just want to dance! Why should I study all this medicine stuff? I already know I want to be a dancer!"

"Nian, you never know where your life will lead you!"

As Linlin is speaking, Nian stands up to test his ankle. He spreads his arms gracefully, leaning forward to put weight on his ankle, and he frowns from the pain.

"Actually, Bian Que's story is pretty impressive, and maybe it's more important for you than you think. You may as well sit down and listen while you rest your ankle," says Linlin. Nian sits down and starts to sulk.

Linlin smiles and says, "Great! So, he began life working at an inn for wealthy travelers. A quiet elderly gentleman stayed for several nights, and, long before he learned about medicine, Bian Que took such good care of the guest that the gentleman decided to reward him by passing on his knowledge. He gave Bian Que many books on medicine and told him to study them. He also gave him a mysterious package of powder, which he was told to mix with water and then drink."

"Bian Que followed the old man's instructions, and, thirty days later, he was amazed to find that his eyes had changed and that he could see inside bodies. Over the following years, Bian Que walked across China using his X-ray vision to diagnose and treat both rich and poor people. He used herbs and performed acupuncture, massage, and surgery."

"OK, Mom, that's a nice fairy tale, but X-ray vision is something for superheroes in comic books, not humans!"

"Maybe 'X-ray vision' is just a way to explain that he could see problems in the body that others couldn't perceive," Linlin suggests.

"OK," says Nian, looking less defiant. "Give me an example."

"Well, when Bian Que was in the state of Cai Ban, he visited the ruler in his castle. The moment he entered the great hall, he could see that the ruler was sick. 'You are lucky, sir. Your sickness is only skin deep. It's not too late to treat it,' he said. But the ruler was distrustful and replied, 'You just want my money. I feel perfectly fine.'"

"The next time Bian Que visited the ruler, he told him sadly that the disease had entered into his blood. 'Nonsense!' the ruler replied. 'The only thing upsetting me is your stories. Stop bothering me, you annoying doctor!' When Bian Que returned the next time, he could see that the disease was now in the ruler's stomach. 'Sir, if you don't let me treat you, I am afraid this will end badly for you!' 'Oh, stop it!' said the ruler. 'I think I can tell whether I am sick or not. It's my body after all, and I feel fine!'"

"He was right. If someone says they feel fine, the doctor should leave them alone," says Nian.

"Well," continues Linlin, "the last time Bian Que visited, he entered the great hall, and when he saw the ruler, he gasped and walked straight out again. The ruler sent his servants after him to ask why he had left, and Bian Que explained to them, 'When the disease was only skin deep, I could have treated it easily with my herbs and powders. But now it has reached right into his bones, and I can do nothing.' Bian Que left the court with great sadness, and the ruler died later that day."

Nian is starting to pay attention: "Interesting, but do you have any stories with happy endings?"

"Yes, this one is almost the opposite. When Bian Que was visiting the state of Guo, he found all the people out in the streets crying. 'What has happened here?' asked Bian Que. 'Our great ruler died in his sleep,' they replied. There was something strange about the way they described the death of their ruler, so Bian Que asked if he could see the body. They led him to where the body lay, and Bian Que noticed right away that the body was warm. After examination, he was able to see that the ruler was not dead at all, but in a coma. He used all his knowledge of acupuncture and herbs to bring the ruler back to health, and, within a month, he was cured."

"Those are cool stories, but I don't see how they're important for my dancing."

Linlin raises her eyes up to the sky. "Come on. It's common sense! Bian Que was famous for listening to the bodies of his patients and seeing what was wrong. He treated the whole person, thinking about their energy level, what they ate, and their daily life."

"Yeah, that makes sense. As a dancer I guess I should see my body like that."

Linlin smiles, pleased to see that her son is starting to understand. "Exactly! What you put into your body is what you get out of it: cut down on junk food, get enough sleep every night, stretch well before exercising. You have to understand how to take care of your body if it's going to be so important for your dancing career."

"OK, so where do I start?" asks Nian, suddenly a little more enthusiastic.

"Well," replies Linlin, "Bian Que was probably the first doctor to sense that the body had a circulatory system. He called it *chi*, meaning the circulation of energy and blood around the body. He could tell a lot about a patient's health just from listening to their pulse. You can start by learning how to take your pulse. You can find it in your wrist or neck. Let's try the wrist. Hold out your hand, palm facing up." Linlin demonstrates with her wrist, and Nian copies her. "Now, we press the index and middle finger on the wrist right below your thumb. You only need to press lightly to feel the pulse. Ah, there it is. Now we count the number of beats we can feel in 60 seconds. Most people have a resting pulse of between 60 and 100 beats per minute."

They check Nian's pulse, and it comes out as 45. "Whoa, mine is much lower!" says Nian. "I'm not sick, am I?"

"Don't worry," Linlin smiles, "it's lower because you are in such good shape. When you check your pulse, you are feeling the blood being pumped around your body by your heart. One of the ways I could tell that you had been dancing earlier was that your pulse was very fast."

Linlin notices Nian is still rubbing his ankle. "Anyway, how's your ankle?"

"Fine, I just sprained it."

"Well, you know Bian Que probably could have helped you with that, too. He was an expert in acupuncture."

"Oh, really, tell me more!" says Nian.

"Acupuncture has existed for 5,000 years. It involves putting needles as thin as single hairs into certain parts of the body to treat problems with the body's *chi*. People say acupuncture can help heal your pain and give you energy, too. One of its uses is to relieve muscle pain and stiff joints, so, as you can imagine, it comes in pretty handy for dancers!"

"Thanks Mom, that's so interesting!" says Nian. "So, can we get some acupuncture for my ankle now?"

Linlin smiles at her son's enthusiasm. "I'll do some research. In the meantime, you can write all this down, and please try to stay in your chair this time!"

"OK, deal!" says Nian.

Key Words

1 Complete the sentences with the Key Words.

a You can take your _____ on your wrist or your neck.

b If you sprain your ankle, try to _____ it with your hands.

c Thin needles are used to perform _____.

d When someone is in a _____, you cannot wake them up.

e I _____ that someone has been in my room, but I can't be sure.

f The students were very _____ and couldn't wait to go on the field trip.

g Dogs can _____ sounds that are too high pitched for humans to hear.

Comprehension

2 Circle the correct options.

a Nian sprained his ankle while he was **studying / dancing / rubbing** it.

b Bian Que's four-step method is for **diagnosing people / giving acupuncture / taking herbal medicine**.

c Bian Que uses his "X-ray vision" to **look through people / make predictions / detect illnesses**.

d In Guo, Bian Que knew the ruler was in a coma because **the story of his death was strange / his body was warm / of the way the body was lying**.

e Nian's pulse rate is lower than average because he **has a sprained ankle / is unhealthy / is healthy**.

f By the end of the story, Nian is **sulking / in great pain / enthusiastic**.

3 Read the observations and write the character from the story they refer to.

a The disease has progressed from your blood to your stomach. _____

b His body is warm. I'll need to perform acupuncture. _____

c Your face is red and sweaty and your pulse is fast! _____

4 How does Linlin use the four-step method to conclude that Nian has been dancing?

Appearance	Breathing	Feeling	Pulse

Digging Deeper

5 🔊 Write notes about two ideas from the story that you found surprising. Complete the graphic organizer.

Before I Read	While I Read	After I Read
I thought that	I was surprised that	Now I think that
I didn't think that	I found that	Now I think maybe

6 Answer the questions.

a In addition to the four-step method, how does Linlin know that Nian was dancing?

_____

b How did the elderly gentleman know that Bian Que would be a good doctor?

_____

c How does the story of the ruler from Cai Ban demonstrate Bian Que's "X-ray" vision?

_____

d How does Linlin convince Nian that the story of Bian Que is important for him?

_____

Personalization

7 Think of a physical activity you like doing (e.g., dancing, swimming, playing soccer). Write three ways to take care of your body for that activity.

Cut down on junk food.

_____

_____

_____

7 Why do we need medicine?

Key Words

1 Preview the Key Words.
7.3

| effective | widespread | theorize | annually | microbiologist |

| industry | frigid | waterproof | technique | medieval |

2 **Replace the words in bold with the correct form of the Key Words.**

a I'm not jumping in that lake. The water is **extremely cold**. _____

b This epidemic is terrible. The disease is **everywhere**. _____

c Herbs were used in lots of **1,000-year-old** cures for illnesses. _____

d Some people get a flu vaccine **every year**. _____

e Acupuncture is **very successful** for my back pain. _____

f This jacket is great. It's warm and **doesn't let the rain in**. _____

g The microbiologist **thought** that the bacteria might be a new species.

_____

h She has to improve her **method of playing** to be a better violinist. _____

Pre-reading

3 **Read the title and subtitles and look at the pictures on pages 107–11. Answer the questions.**

a What problem do you think the text talks about?

_____

b Where do you think we can find possible solutions?

_____

4 **Listen and read.**
7.4

Antibiotics of the Future?

By Nicola Pitt

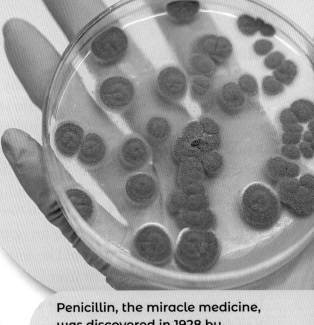

Miracle Medicine

Did you know that penicillin was called the "miracle medicine"? That's because it was the world's first antibiotic. Infectious diseases were the main cause of death in the world when penicillin was discovered. And antibiotics like penicillin could treat some of those diseases. Before then, you could easily die from a disease like pneumonia. For a lung infection like that, the best advice doctors had was to get some fresh air!

Penicillin, the miracle medicine, was discovered in 1928 by Alexander Fleming. It comes from penicillin mold like this.

Alexander Fleming in his laboratory

Even an ordinary cut on your skin could be life-threatening. Our skin protects us against bacteria, but a scratch can get infected easily. In the First World War, many people survived getting shot, but died when their wounds became infected. Doctors could do little except hope that their patients would get better. Antibiotics changed all of that.

The Emergence of the Superbugs!

But, now, antibiotics are less effective. That's because they are so widely used. They are so widespread that they are even in the food we eat! Many farmers feed their cows and other livestock antibiotics to keep them healthy. That means that humans take medicine every time they eat meat. And, if we take antibiotics when they aren't necessary, or if we don't complete an antibiotic treatment, then bacteria can become resistant to antibiotics. These bacteria are often called "superbugs."

MRSA is one kind of superbug.

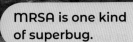

Life Without Antibiotics?

Scientists theorize that by 2050 many antibiotics will not work anymore because bacteria will evolve to become resistant to them. That means that infections could be the main cause of death in the world. People could easily die from diseases like pneumonia once again. Superbugs could cause 10 million deaths annually! If we don't have antibiotics that work, routine surgery, like removing an appendix, would be very dangerous. And it would be impossible to replace an organ like the heart or liver.

In the future, people might not say hello with a hug or handshake. They might be too scared of germs! Would we stop taking public transportation if infectious diseases become so deadly again? Could hobbies like skateboarding become too dangerous because a simple scratch could get infected by dangerous bacteria?

A future without skateboarding?

The Race Against the Superbugs

A future without antibiotics (and skateboarding!) looks bad. So why don't we have any new antibiotics? The main reason is that it's very expensive to develop them. We don't use antibiotics as much as other drugs, so drug companies don't make very much money producing and selling antibiotics. In fact, the last new antibiotic was discovered in 1987! Fortunately, governments and universities across the world are supporting research that may help us in the race against the superbugs!

Much of that research is being done by microbiologists. They are scientists who investigate microscopic organisms. They often work in hospitals and universities. You'll even find them in the space industry! They study bacteria, so they know the most about infectious diseases and how to stop them. And they're looking in the rainforests, under the ocean, and even into ancient medicine for new types of antibiotics.

A microbiologist at work

Rainforest Remedies

Most antibiotics come from the soil, and scientists from Rutgers University in the United States are studying the soil in a Mexican rainforest. They discovered unusual bacteria living on the roots of a bean plant. These friendly bacteria produce an antibiotic that protects the bean plant from harmful bacteria. Scientists think that these unusual bacteria will be useful for growing beans, peas, lentils, and peanuts. They also theorize that they will work against bacteria that harm people.

Where will the next antibiotics come from? From the rainforest soil?

Underwater Cures?

Not a single antibiotic has ever come from the ocean! In the early days of antibiotic research, scuba diving was dangerous, so nobody looked for antibiotics. But now that new discoveries in soil are rare, scientists are looking underwater for new medicine.

Brian Murphy, a scientist from Chicago, is studying the ocean around Iceland! He thinks that he might discover new types of life there. And, there might be new medicine just waiting to be found, too. But it's not easy work. To go diving in the frigid waters around Iceland, you can't just wear a wetsuit. Instead, Murphy has to wear warm clothes and socks underneath a dry suit. It's made of a thick waterproof material. Then, he can collect organisms and put them into test tubes to test whether they can work as antibiotics. Perhaps one of these test tubes from the Icelandic ocean will contain the next great antibiotic!

From the frigid waters of Iceland?

The Ancient Wisdom of the Druids

Could any answers be hidden in Irish soil? There is a grassy area in Ireland where druids lived 1,500 years ago. A druid was a kind of ancient healer or magician. Since the time of the druids, some people have believed that the soil from this area can cure infections. They would wrap a small amount of the soil in cotton. Then, they put it next to an infection or even underneath the patient's pillow for nine days. This technique was used for many ailments, like toothaches and throat infections!

Will the next antibiotics come from soil that druids thought could cure infections?

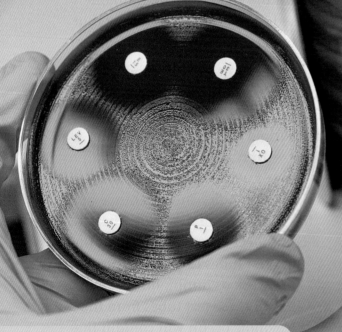

A microbiologist testing antibiotics

Now scientists from Swansea University are studying that soil to see if the druids' cures work. And guess what? They have discovered a new type of bacteria in it. Their tests show that it works against four superbugs! Professor Paul Dyson said, "Our results show that folklore and traditional medicines are worth investigating in the search for new antibiotics. ... It seems that part of the answer to this very modern problem might lie in the wisdom of the past."[1]

[1] Swansea University. "Bacteria found in ancient Irish soil halts growth of superbugs: New hope for tackling antibiotic resistance." ScienceDaily. www.sciencedaily.com/releases/2018/12/181227111427.htm (accessed February 14, 2020).

A Medieval Cure for Modern Superbugs?

It is also possible that we've found a new antibiotic thanks to a book of medieval cures. *The Leechbook*, in the British Library, is one of the oldest medical textbooks in the world. It contains recipes for medicines that were used 1,000 years ago in England. One remedy for eye infections includes ingredients like garlic and onions! Microbiologists from the University of Nottingham recreated the ancient remedy to see if it works as an antibiotic.

Or will the next antibiotics be found in a medieval textbook?

The next miracle medicine?

They were surprised to discover that it seems to be more effective than normal antibiotics for treating superbugs! "I still can't quite believe how well this 1,000-year-old antibiotic actually seems to be working. … We did not see this coming at all. … The potential of this … is just beyond my wildest dreams," said Dr. Freya Harrison.[2]

The Future of Antibiotics

Whether we look in the rainforests, under the ocean, or at the past for future cures, these discoveries sound promising. In the meantime, we should be careful to take antibiotics responsibly. Maybe then, we won't even need new miracle medicines!

2 Mike Barrett. "Scientists Discover All-Natural Medieval Potion Kills Superbugs & Infections That Antibiotics Can't." Conscious Life News. www.consciouslifenews.com/scientists-discover-all-natural-medieval-potion-kills-superbugs-infections-anti-biotics/1183084/#. (accessed February 14, 2020).

Key Words

1 Complete the sentences with the pairs of Key Words.

| microbiologist/theorized   industry/effective   widespread/annually |
| waterproof/frigid   medieval/technique |

a The drug _____ has researched many _____ medicines, but it is expensive.

b My wetsuit was _____, but I still felt cold in the _____ water.

c One _____ _____ was called trepanning, or cutting a hole in the skull.

d Louis Pasteur was a _____ who _____ that microorganisms are the causes of diseases.

e Flu is a _____ illness and occurs _____, usually in the winter.

Comprehension

2 Circle the correct options.

1 What was the world's first antibiotic?
   a bacteria   b bean plants   c penicillin

2 What is a characteristic of a superbug?
   a It comes from meat.   b It is resistant to antibiotics.   c It stops us from saying "hello" to people.

3 Where has an antibiotic never been found?
   a in soil   b in old textbooks   c in the ocean

4 What do the antibiotics from "Rainforest Remedies" and "The Ancient Wisdom of the Druids" have in common?
   a They come from the soil. b They come from Mexico. c They involve magic.

5 What is *The Leechbook* about?
   a microbiology   b cooking   c medieval medicine

3 Match the ideas to the areas of research.

1 Old techniques for curing toothaches can be effective against superbugs.

2 Friendly bacteria that protect plants might also protect people.

3 Recipes that include garlic and onions can work as antibiotics.

4 If we find new types of life, we might find new types of medicine.

a underwater cures

b druid beliefs

c rainforests

d medieval cures

Digging Deeper

4 📖 **Complete the chain of causes and effects to answer the question.**

How might scientists have found new antibiotics in the Mexican rainforest?
Cause: Scientists from Rutgers University in the United States studied the soil in a Mexican rainforest.

a **Effect:** They discovered _____ living on the roots of a _____.

b **Effect:** They realized these _____ bacteria _____ the bean plants from harmful bacteria.

c **Effect:** The scientists theorize that they will work against bacteria that _____ people.

5 **Choose two of the subsections of the article and summarize how antibiotics were or might be found by the researchers.**

Subsection Title: _____   Subsection Title: _____

_____   _____

_____   _____

_____   _____

_____   _____

Personalization

6 **In the conclusion, the text says, "we should be careful to take antibiotics responsibly."** **Write one piece of advice for how to use antibiotics responsibly.**

_____

_____

_____

7 **Be creative and theorize another source of future antibiotics. Why might your source be a good one?**

_____

_____

_____

8 How do we use money?

Key Words

1 🎧 **Preview the Key Words.**

 ordeal

 novice

 expert

 disheartened

 industrious

 set up (v)

 infuriating

 ridiculous

 imaginary

 request (v)

2 **Match the Key Words to their opposites.**

1	novice	a	motivated
2	disheartened	b	real
3	industrious	c	take down
4	infuriating	d	pleasant activity
5	ridiculous	e	lazy
6	imaginary	f	serious
7	set up	g	expert
8	ordeal	h	pleasing

Pre-reading

3 📖 **Look at the title and pictures on pages 115–21. Circle the possible themes of the story.**

heroism   helpfulness   anger   jealousy

friendship   patience

4 🎧 **Listen and read.**

Woogle Zoo

By S. Bastian Harris • Illustrated by Berenice Muñiz

BOOM!

School can be such an ordeal. I had THREE tests! But now I'm home, and that means it's time to relax and play Woogle Zoo!

It's the latest, greatest new game. Everyone at school is playing it! Ms. Garrows, my social studies teacher, recommended it. She told everyone it's a fantastic way to learn about money. My parents aren't so sure, but it is pretty fun.

Your Money $50
Visitors: 0

Catie's Zoo

Welcome back to Planet Woogle!

You have 50 Woogle dollars!

Do you want to improve your zoo?

YE

SIGH ...

**ALERT:
You need more funds!
Buy more
Woogle dollars now?**

YES   NO

I'm a novice. I just started playing yesterday, but there are some kids who are experts. They've been playing it all year. You should see their zoos! It'll take forever to catch up with them.

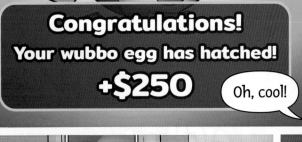

Now I have 1,800 Woogle dollars!

 Create a new exhibit. $325

 Add a fence. $150

 Add a pool. $225

 Open a gift shop. $750

Buy new animals. $$$

Look at all these options!

I added a pool for the wubboes; I bought a rainbow zeeble; and I put in a gift shop! My zoo was beautiful!

Your money $325
Visitors: 0

Catie's Zoo

DING!

You've unlocked zoo jobs!
Work at your zoo
to make more cash!

YES   NO

$45 + $15 + $20 = ?

Look how industrious
I am! I made $200 working
at the gift shop.

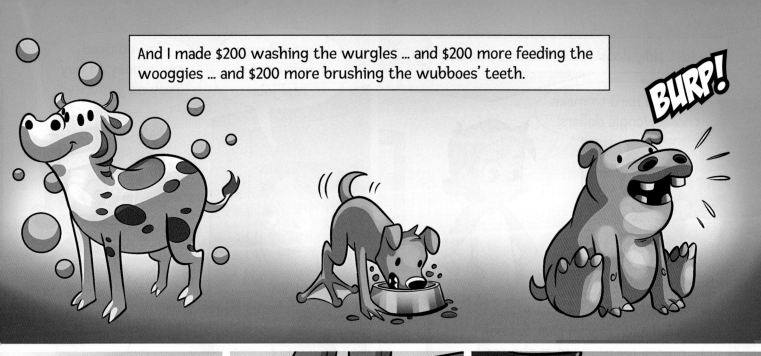

119

121

Key Words

1 **Circle the word that doesn't belong**

a busy, industrious, inactive, hard-working

b test, comfort, ordeal, nightmare

c novice, authority, professional, expert

d request, ask, inquire, answer

e irritating, fascinating, infuriating, aggravating

f funny, serious, silly, ridiculous

g pretend, imaginary, real, fantasy

h frustrated, discouraged, enthusiastic, disheartened

Comprehension

2 **Read the story again and number the events in order.**

☐ Amy tells Catie that she can make Woogle dollars by getting friends to sign up for the game.

☐ Catie can't buy any Woogle dollars and has to wait until a wubbo egg hatches.

☐ Catie starts playing the game but realizes she needs more funds.

☐ Grandpa and Grandma offer Catie real money to help them.

☐ It takes a long time to make Catie's mom's zoo nice after Catie agrees to help her set it up.

☐ Mom requests help from Catie, but Catie is jealous because her mom used real money to buy Woogle dollars.

☐ Mom, Grandpa, and Grandma start playing, and Catie makes more money.

☐ Ms. Garrows recommends a game that helps players learn about money.

3 **Write the result for each of the actions.**

a Action: Catie waits for three days.

Result: _____

b Action: She sends out lots of invitations.

Result: _____

c Action: She unlocks zoo jobs.

Result: _____

d Action: She helps her mom set up her zoo.

Result: _____

Digging Deeper

4 📖 **Read and match the story extracts with the themes.**

1 I need your help. Can you show me how to improve my zoo? I have to spend all these Woogle dollars now.	**a patience**
2 So now Mom is one of the richest people on Planet Woogle. And she didn't even have to work for it! It's so infuriating!!!	**b helpfulness**
3 So I waited. And waited. And waited. I couldn't buy anything for three days!	**c jealousy**

5 📖 **Complete the diagram.**

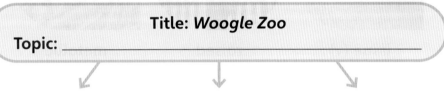

Title: *Woogle Zoo*

Topic: _____

What happens in the story as part of this topic?

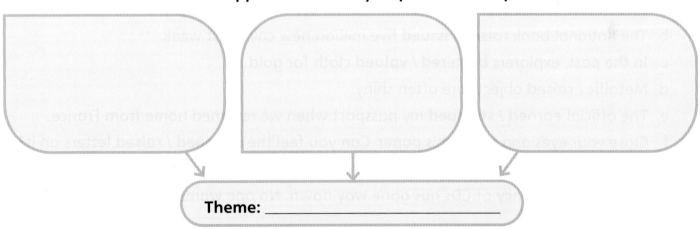

Theme: _____

Personalization

6 **Write notes in the table about a game you know of that helps you learn things.**

Name of Game:
What It Helps You Learn:

8 How do we use money?

Key Words

1 🎧 **Preview the Key Words.**
8.3

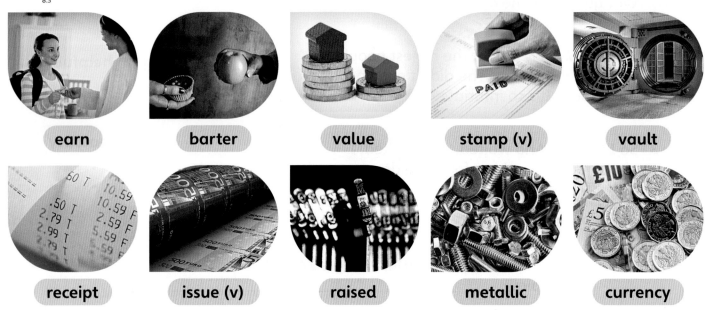

| earn | barter | value | stamp (v) | vault |

| receipt | issue (v) | raised | metallic | currency |

2 **Circle the correct options.**

a I wash cars on the weekend to **earn** / **barter** some extra money.

b The national bank **raised** / **issued** five million new coins last week.

c In the past, explorers **bartered** / **valued** cloth for gold.

d **Metallic** / **raised** objects are often shiny.

e The official **earned** / **stamped** my passport when we returned home from France.

f Close your eyes and touch this paper. Can you feel the **stamped** / **raised** letters on it?

g You need to take the **vault** / **receipt** with you to return that shirt at the store.

h The **value** / **currency** of CDs has gone way down. No one wants to buy them anymore.

Pre-reading

3 **Look at the subtitles, pictures, and captions on pages 125–29. Make predictions about what people used, use now, or will use as money.**

In the Past	Today	In the Future

4 🎧 **Listen and read.**
8.4

MONEY MAKES THE WORLD GO AROUND

By Garan Holcombe

Some spend it, others save it, celebrities earn a lot of it, and life isn't very easy without it. We're talking about money, of course. But what is money, how did it develop, how is it made, how do we stop criminals from making fake money, and how is it changing?

What Is Money?

Money is anything that we can use to pay for the things we buy. Today this is usually cash or electronic money. But a variety of things have been used throughout history, such as cowrie shells in Africa and Asia, cocoa beans in Central America, and arrowheads in Europe. In Tibet, they once used blocks of dried tea!

Cowrie shells

Arrowheads

Cacao beans

That'll Be Three Deerskins, Please!

Before we invented money, we used to barter. If you wanted some grain, for example, you might offer someone a deerskin for it. But this only worked if the other person had what you wanted and wanted what you had. And how could you know if a deerskin was worth the same as a kilogram of grain?

In the Middle East, in about 9,000 BCE, people began to agree on the value of things. They decided how many stone tools or pieces of pottery could be bought with a cow, an animal valued for its meat and milk. This was the beginning of "commodity money"—money that was valued because of what it was made out of.

Fun Money Fact!
The word "money" comes from the Latin *moneda*, which was a name given to the goddess Juno by the Romans. Money was made in her temple!

From the 4th century BCE to the 20th century CE, Chinese coins had square holes in their center. Today, people in China think these coins are good-luck symbols.

A Short History of Coins

The first coins were made, or minted, in Lydia (in modern-day Turkey) about 2,700 years ago. They were made from gold and silver and stamped with images of lions, owls, or snakes. Over time, coins spread around the world. Governments used them to collect taxes from people.

Fun Money Fact!
Not all coins are or were round. Square coins were minted in India around 2,400 years ago!

At first, the value of a coin was connected to what it was made of. Gold and silver were rare metals, so coins made out of them were valuable. But coins were too heavy to carry around in large quantities, easy to steal, and people started to make fake ones. They mixed gold and silver with less valuable metals to make copies of the gold and silver coins, and then they would use them as if they were real.

There was another problem: metals, such as gold and silver, were much too valuable to use for everyday purchases, so coins started to be made from less valuable metals, such as bronze, copper, and zinc.

Governments make coins in special factories called mints.

Today, a coin can cost more to produce than it is worth! For that reason, in 2012, the Canadian government stopped making the one-cent piece. It's not the only country that has done it. Over the last few decades, the U.K., Spain, New Zealand, and other countries have stopped minting some of their smallest coins.

Since they were first made in Lydia, coins have kept some of the same features. They are still stamped with a special design, and they show where they are from. Modern coins also show the value of the coin and the year it was made.

Fun Money Fact!
The largest gold coin in the world was made in Australia in 2012. It is worth 1 million Australian dollars, is 80 cm in diameter and 13 cm thick, and weighs 1,012 kg! Try carrying that in your pocket!

The Invention of Paper Money

Carrying lots of heavy coins around was a problem, but the bankers of tenth-century China solved this problem by using their country's paper-making and printing technologies. In return for storing people's coins in secure places called vaults, they gave out paper receipts that showed how many coins people had in the vault. These receipts could then be used to pay for things. Anyone who received a paper receipt could take it to the vault and collect the coins.

These receipts were the world's first bills, but they were only used for large quantities of money. But there was a new problem: they were much easier to copy, or counterfeit, than coins. For this reason, it took a long time for bills to be accepted widely in China and around the world.

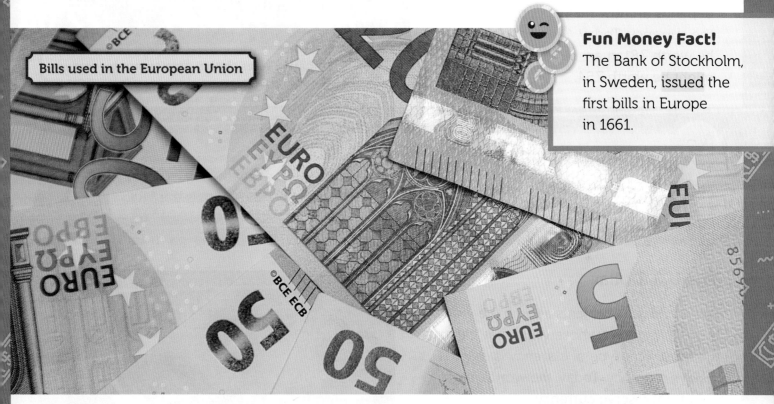

Bills used in the European Union

Fun Money Fact!
The Bank of Stockholm, in Sweden, issued the first bills in Europe in 1661.

Stopping the Criminals

Bills are issued by governments or central banks. (A central bank is a bank that helps a government run all of the banking of the country.) To make it harder for people to copy them, these bills have complicated designs. They use raised print—if you touch the bill, you can feel the raised areas. They also use metallic threads, which appear as single lines when you hold the bill up to the light, a design called a watermark, which you can also only see in the light, and an image called a hologram, which changes when you move the bill.

A real or fake Mongolian bill?

How Much Is That in Pesos?

The money a country uses is called its
currency. The yuan is China's currency,
while nineteen countries in Europe
use a currency called the euro. If you
want to exchange yuan for euros, you
need to know the exchange rate: that's
the value of the yuan in comparison to
the value of the euro. Like the weather,
these values change all the time! It all
depends on how many people want
the currency. Today, 1 euro might
be worth 7.81 yuan, but tomorrow it
might be worth 7.54.

🇺🇸 **USD** 50-100	30.35	31.55
🇪🇺 **EUR**	34.24	35.50
🇭🇰 **HKD**	3.73	0.00
🇬🇧 **GBP**	38.70	39.90
🇸🇬 **SGD**	22.64	0.00
🇯🇵 **JPY**	0.2719	0.2824
🇦🇺 **AUD**	21.41	22.04

Exchange rates shown on a computer screen

Fun Money Fact!

Every currency in the world has its own three-letter abbreviation, e.g., the U.S.
dollar is the USD, the Mexican peso is the MXN, and the Turkish lira is the TRY.

The U.S. Dollar

Banks and governments around the world
buy the currency whose value they can trust
the most. This type of currency is called a
reserve currency. Today, the world's most
important reserve currency is the U.S. dollar,
but, one day, it might be China's yuan.

Say Goodbye to Gold

In the 19th and 20th centuries, the value of
a currency was linked to gold. That meant
that you could exchange $20 for $20 worth
of gold. In 1971, however, the last country
(the U.S.) to link the value of money to gold
stopped doing it. Since then, we have had
"fiat money." *Fiat* is a Latin word and means

Gold bars, which are called ingots

"let it be done." The coins and bills in our wallets aren't linked to anything at all. They are
valuable only because the government says that they are, and we behave like they are!

Electronic Money

Today, many of us use electronic money such as debit cards, credit cards, and smartphone apps to pay for things in stores. We use the Internet to pay bills and go online to buy everything from clothes to books. The big question is this: will any countries become cashless in the next twenty years?

Paying with a credit or debit card is becoming more and more common.

Fun Money Fact!

People on the island of Yap in Micronesia don't use electronic money or cash. For centuries, they have been using large stones as money. Found all over the island, most of the stones are too big to move and can be up to 3.6 meters across!

Are Cryptocurrencies the Future?

A cryptocurrency is a digital currency that is sent directly from one user to another on a computer or electronic device. Cyptocurrencies are not controlled or supported by a government or a central bank. Bitcoin is the most well-known cryptocurrency. You get Bitcoins by buying them from someone or by using a powerful computer to break a complicated code. If you crack the code, you are rewarded with new bitcoins.

Bitcoin became the world's first cryptocurrency in 2009.

Bitcoin is very safe: there is a record of every Bitcoin that's ever been created and every time someone has used one. It makes it very hard to produce counterfeit Bitcoins.

But there are problems. The value of Bitcoin has gone up and down over the last few years; you can't exchange Bitcoins for another currency at a bank; they are difficult to get; and you can't spend them in many places. But some people think that cryptocurrencies are the future. What about you? How do you think money will change?

Key Words

1 **Read the definitions and write the Key Words.**

a what something is worth; the price of something _____

b a piece of paper that shows how much money you either paid or have

_____

c the money that a country uses _____

d to make something, like money, available to use _____

e a secure room to store things and keep them safe _____

f to exchange products and services for other products and services (without money)

_____

Comprehension

2 **Read the text again and circle the correct options.**

1 What is money?

   a shells, beans, and arrowheads   b anything we use to pay for things   c coins

2 When were the first coins made?

   a 9,000 BCE   b 4th century BCE   c 2,700 years ago

3 What is the main reason some countries stop making some coins?

   a They are heavy.   b They are easy to steal.   c They are expensive to produce.

4 What was the new problem with paper money when it was invented?

   a It was easy to copy.   b It was only available in China.   c It was only for large quantities.

5 What affects the value of a currency?

   a the weather   b how many people want it   c the size of the country

6 How is cryptocurrency similar to other currencies?

   a It is cashless.   b It is only used on the Internet.   c Its value goes up and down.

3 **Match the sentences to the topics.**

1 I'll give you a chicken for three kilos of grain.   a exchange rate

2 That watermark is very difficult to see.   b bartering

3 One euro is worth about 1.10 dollars.   c cryptocurrency

4 I use my card to pay bills online!   d counterfeit bills

5 There is a record of every time it is used.   e counterfeit coins

6 Less valuable metals were mixed in.   f electronic money

Digging Deeper

4 📖 Which questions are answered directly in the text and which do you have to infer the answers to? Complete the chart, quoting from the text where possible.

Question	Answer	Direct or Inferred
a Were all coins round?		
b What are the three-letter abbreviations for the currencies of the United States, Mexico, and Turkey?		
c What is a cryptocurrency?		
d Why do people use electronic money such as debit cards, credit cards, and smartphone apps to pay for things?		

5 Write three more questions you can answer by quoting from the text.

a _____

b _____

c _____

6 Write the direct quotations from the text that answer the questions in Activity 5.

a _____

b _____

c _____

Personalization

7 Answer the questions.

a Which "Fun Money Fact" did you find the most interesting and why?

_____

b Do you think cryptocurrencies are the future of money? Why or why not?

_____

9 How can we increase our brainpower?

Key Words

1 🎧 Preview the Key Words.
9.1

nickname reminder slightly confirm vaguely

coincidence speculate scold gossip (v) hideous

2 Complete the sentences with the correct form of the Key Words.

a His real name is Charles, but his _____ is Chuck.

b It was the ugliest painting I have ever seen. It was _____!

c I can't believe we bought the same jacket. What a _____!

d Dad _____ me for making a mess in my room. He made me clean it up.

e The invitations asked the guests to _____ that they were coming to the party.

f Can you send me a _____ so that I don't forget my doctor's appointment?

Pre-reading

3 Look at the pictures on pages 133–41 and make predictions.

a Who are the main characters?

_____

b Where does the story take place?

_____

c What do you think the mystery is?

_____

4 🎧 Listen and read.
9.2

THE MYSTERY AT THE SCHOOL FAIR

By Jenna Briggs-Fish • Illustrated by Mario Garza

Edmund Bigglesworth and his younger sister, Tori, live at 12 Mustard Lane. Edmund's nickname is Biggles, and, over the years, Biggles and his sister have been close friends with their neighbors, Darsha and Raj. Darsha Chaudhry is eleven, a year younger than Biggles. And Darsha's brother, Raj, is nine—he's the youngest of the four friends.

Despite their different ages, the four friends love to fight crime together, but not in a pretend, superhero kind of way; no, these four friends love being detectives. Over the last few years, they have started to call themselves the Smart Four. Many people might think that to be a detective you need to be super smart. Well, these kids are, that's why they chose the name the Smart Four. But you won't find them getting As on a math test or winning a spelling bee. With Biggles's guidance, they've developed other useful skills, like conversational skills and the art of observation. They see what most of us don't. And it's thanks to these skills that they've solved several local mysteries.

THE SMART FOUR

Their most recent success happened by chance. It was the winter fair at their school. It was a typical winter's day, and Biggles and Tori were wearing their warmest jackets. When they got to the fair, they found Darsha and Raj by a game called Hook-A-Duck.

"Did you win anything yet?" Biggles asked them.

"Not me, but Raj just won a goldfish," said Tori.

"I'm going to call it Bubbles," said Raj excitedly.

"Don't get too attached to it," Darsha warned him. "You don't even know if Mom will let you keep it."

"Come on. How hard can it be to take care of a fish? It's not like a dog or a rabbit," he answered, a little annoyed.

"Have you guys been to the bouncy house yet?" asked Tori hopefully.

"No, but I have to go help Mom run her stand." Darsha replied. "Why don't you and Raj go ahead, and I'll find you when I've finished."

"In the meantime, I'm going to take a look around," said Biggles.

Darsha, who knew him very well, wasn't fooled. "Biggles, I think we can have a day off from detective work, can't we? It's the school fair. What could happen here?"

"You never know," said Biggles.

A little later, Darsha was serving her math teacher a samosa and soda pop at her mom's stand. "That'll be three dollars and fifty cents, please," she said to him.

"It's good to see that you're practicing your math skills, Darsha," he said. It sounded to Darsha like her teacher thought she never practiced math.

"Yes. Thank you, Mr. Tripp," replied Darsha, smiling innocently. She knew math wasn't her strongest subject, but did she really need a reminder on the weekend? Just then, her mother came back to the stand looking slightly confused.

"Is everything alright, Mom?" she asked.

"I guess so. Only Mrs. Button can't find a spool of pink ribbon she had at her stand," her mother explained. "She keeps complaining it just disappeared."

"How strange! Do you think someone stole it?" Darsha asked.

Stolen?

"You kids read too many crime novels!" her mom said. "She probably just left it at home. You don't need to make something out of nothing, Darsha."

But, Darsha wasn't convinced. Mrs. Button's use of the word "disappeared" seemed strange to her, so, as soon as she could, she snuck over to Mrs. Button's stand to question the lady herself. Her interview confirmed her suspicions; Mrs. Button couldn't have left the ribbon at home because she had sold two meters of it to Patsy Merkle's twins earlier that morning, and, despite looking in every box, the ribbon couldn't be found. Wasn't that suspicious?

At 2 p.m., Darsha found Tori and Raj who had bounced themselves in the bouncy house almost to exhaustion. Now they were starving.

"Let's go get a slice of apple pie and some hot chocolate," suggested Darsha. "I'll pay!"

"Did someone say apple pie?"

They turned around to find Biggles smiling.

"It's just like you to hear 'apple pie' and come running," Darsha joked.

"Actually, I have something that might interest you guys. It looks like there's work for the Smart Four after all," said Biggles.

"What? What is it?" cried Raj and Tori eagerly.

Biggles explained that he had been standing near Mrs. Cotton's stand with knitted crafts, where she was selling everything from oversized sweaters to toys vaguely resembling exotic animals, when he heard something that made him curious. Mrs. Cotton was complaining to Dr. Chen that her favorite sweater had disappeared. Apparently, she had put it out on her stand when she arrived, but now it wasn't there.

"Is anyone helping her at her stand? Maybe they sold it and forgot to tell her," suggested Raj, trying to be realistic.

"That's what I thought, but the only person helping her is her sister, and it turns out she hasn't sold any sweaters today. Isn't that strange?"

"The mystery of the missing sweater. Well, that's a case we haven't solved before," Tori teased her brother.

"You can joke if you want," replied Biggles, "but I think this could be worth investigating. We might have a thief at the fair."

"I'm afraid, Biggles might be right," admitted Darsha, and went on to tell them about Mrs. Button's missing ribbon.

"What does that magazine *Detective Mastermind* always say?" Biggles reminded them. "There are no coincidences."

Investigating a case once again, the Smart Four speculated about the possible explanations as they made their way to get some apple pie. They arrived just in time to witness an argument between Mrs. Lard and her nephew, Frankie. She was scolding him for eating pie that was supposed to be for sale.

"But I didn't eat any, Aunt!" Frankie pleaded.

"I will tell your mother what a thief you are, Franklin Price!" Mrs. Lard shouted. "Now, get out of here. No more free pie!"

As they watched Frankie leave, the Smart Four glanced at each other. It was time to investigate.

While Biggles and Raj followed Frankie, Darsha and Tori took the opportunity to get more details from Mrs. Lard, who was happy to gossip about her nephew and his endless appetite for pie.

Later, the four met to compare notes. Frankie insisted that he hadn't eaten a single piece of pie, and Biggles believed him. He explained to his friends that he remembered his mom telling him that Frankie was lactose intolerant. When Frankie declined a hot chocolate that Biggles offered him, it confirmed the fact. Besides, if Frankie had eaten the pie, which had whipped cream on it, he'd have a terrible stomachache, but that wasn't the case.

"Well, that fits," Darsha said slowly. "Mrs. Lard admitted that she didn't actually see Frankie eating any pie. Three pieces disappeared, and she just assumed it was him because, as she put it, who else could it be?"

137

"OK," said Biggles, taking control as usual. "The missing things so far are a spool of sparkly, pink ribbon, a sweater, and three pieces of apple pie. Any thoughts?"

"It could be kids messing around," suggested Darsha.

"Maybe, but why would any kid want one of Mrs. Cotton's knitted sweaters? They're hideous," said Tori bluntly.

"True. OK, what if someone didn't want them but needed them instead? A person without a lot of money, perhaps? Maybe they need the sweater to keep warm and took the pie because they were hungry?" Biggles hypothesized.

"Well, hunger and cold are logical motives; it is freezing out here today, but I think people would notice someone walking around in a hideous sweater and carrying three pieces of pie and sparkly, pink ribbon. Besides, you have to pay to enter the fair," Darsha reasoned.

"What if someone inside the fair was stealing the items for someone outside the fair who needed them?" Biggles speculated.

Just then, Tori heard their mom calling. She asked them if they'd seen Betsy Fortuna. Betsy was in first grade at the school. Apparently, she'd arrived at the fair with her mom in the morning, but no one had seen her since. Her mom was now worried because it was getting dark.

"Do you think the thief took Betsy?" Tori asked, horrified. "Maybe he's keeping her warm with the hideous sweater and feeding her pie!"

Biggles looked at his sister; he was unimpressed. "Tori, you're letting your imagination run away with you again. Remember we work with facts and logic, not fiction. Logic tells us that Betsy would have come to the fair wearing a coat, like all of us, so she wouldn't need one of Mrs. Cotton's sweaters. A more likely hypothesis is that Betsy is our thief."

"But if you don't think she's stealing the items for herself, who are they for?" questioned Darsha.

"It would have to be someone she knows," added Raj. "If her mom's like ours, she wouldn't like it if she talked to strangers."

"But, who would she bring to the fair who couldn't come in?" Tori wondered.

Biggles was forced to interrupt them. The fair was almost over. Further speculation would have to wait. If their theory was right and Betsy was outside taking care of someone, they would need to find her before it got dark.

Raj, who had a photographic memory, sketched a map of the school, and together they highlighted possible hiding places. The preschoolers' play area? The bike storage shed? The trees behind the soccer field? The bike storage shed, they agreed, would be the warmest shelter if Betsy and whoever she was with were cold.

It was almost 4 p.m. It would soon be dark, so they had to hurry. Biggles pulled out his flashlight (because no good detective goes anywhere without one) and led the way.

Suddenly, Raj saw something pink twinkling on the ground in the beam of the flashlight.

"Pink sparkles!" He cried getting down on his knees.

"We must be on the right track, then," said Biggles excitedly.

The trail of sparkly dust led them to the bike storage shed, as they predicted. From inside, they could hear a girl's voice. She seemed to be talking to someone. They figured it had to be Betsy, so Darsha, who everyone knew was great at talking to people, volunteered to talk to her.

"Betsy? Is that you?" she said quietly as she approached the little girl huddled in the corner of the freezing cold shed where the bikes were stored.

"You can't take him; he's mine!" Betsy cried out.

As Darsha got closer, everything suddenly made sense. Hidden behind Betsy wasn't a person but a small dog dressed in Mrs. Cotton's sweater. It had a sparkly, pink ribbon tied around its neck as a leash.

"Where did you find him?" asked Darsha kindly.

Betsy hesitated, but replied, "Just outside the school gates. But I'm taking care of him. He's mine now."

"I can see you're doing a great job. Did he like the apple pie?"

Betsy looked down guiltily. Darsha explained that the fair was over and that everyone was leaving. She hoped that Betsy would come with her and take the dog to her mom.

"But she won't let me keep him!" Betsy cried out. "She never lets me have pets."

Darsha managed to reason with her, and soon the girls came out of the bike shed with the dog following on the sparkly leash.

Back at the fair, Betsy's mother was so relieved to be reunited with her daughter. However, she was disappointed in Betsy and made her promise to repay Mrs. Button, Mrs. Cotton, and Mrs. Lard with her allowance. As for the dog, Morgan Dwight, the local vet, offered to find it a home. Betsy was delighted when he said she could visit the dog whenever she liked.

Before she left, Betsy's mother thanked and congratulated the Smart Four. "You four certainly are good at solving mysteries. Have you thought about being detectives when you grow up?"

The Smart Four looked at each other and grinned.

Key Words

1 Read the clues and complete the word puzzle with Key Words. Then, find the hidden word.

1 something that causes you to remember or think about something
2 a little bit
3 to talk about the personal lives of other people
4 to think or wonder about something
5 a name that isn't your real name
6 to say that something is true
7 in an unclear way

Comprehension

2 Complete the sentences with the names of the characters.

a _____ is the leader of the Smart Four.
b _____ helps out at her mom's stand.
c _____ cannot find her favorite sweater.
d _____ insists he didn't eat the pie.
e _____ sees something pink on the ground.
f _____ took the items to take care of a dog.

3 Which strategies did you use to monitor and clarify your understanding of the story? Choose three words or sentences you didn't understand at first and complete the chart.

reread the text   read the words aloud
look for clues in the sentence   use a dictionary   other

I didn't understand:	I used these strategies:	Now I think it means:
a		
b		
c		

Digging Deeper

4 Check your ideas from Activity 3 on page 132. Then, complete the story map.

Setting:	Main Characters:	Supporting Characters:
Event I:	Event 2:	Event 3:
Problem:	Solution:	

5 What skills did each character use to help solve the mystery? Write notes in the chart.

Character	Skill	Example
a Biggles		
b Darsha		
c Raj		

Personalization

6 Could you be one of the Smart Four? Answer the questions.

a What skill do you have that can help solve mysteries?

_____

b Give an example of when you used this skill.

_____

How can we increase our brainpower?

Key Words

1 Preview the Key Words.

 genius

 figure out

 intelligence

 joke

 versatile

 playlist

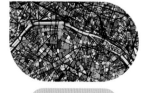 visualize

 detailed

 perspective

cheer up

2 Match.

figure out

genius   **noun**

versatile

perspective   **verb**

cheer up

visualize   **adjective**

detailed

- giving a lot of information
- to finally understand something after thinking about it
- to form a mental picture of something
- the point of view from which you see or think about something
- a very smart person
- able to do many different things
- to stop feeling sad or to make someone feel happier

Pre-reading

3 📖 Look at the title on page 145 and write notes in the chart. Write two or three ideas in each column.

What I Know About Geniuses	What I Want to Know About Geniuses

4 🎧 Listen and read.
9.4

What Kind of Genius Are You?

By Susannah Reed

Do you ever think that other people are smarter than you? Is there someone in your class who always gets the best grade on English assignments? Or is better at math? But have you ever noticed that you are better than they are at finding your way around? This is because people can be smart in different ways. What kind of genius are you?

Are You Good with Numbers?

Do you like solving math problems? Is it easy for you to figure out logic puzzles and riddles? If so, then you have good logical-mathematical intelligence.

People with high logical-mathematical intelligence see patterns and connections between things. They are good at solving problems and making new discoveries. Therefore, they make good scientists and inventors—like Albert Einstein, who lived from 1879 to 1955. Einstein made many very important scientific discoveries, such as the theory of relativity and theories about light. His inventions included a type of refrigerator. Are you the next Albert Einstein?

Improve Your Logical-Mathematical Intelligence

- Play games that use logic or math skills, such as chess or dominoes.
- Visit a science museum and find out about a scientific discovery. Write notes about the effects this discovery has had on the world.
- Create a savings jar for something you really want to buy. Add money to the jar each week. How long will it take you to save enough money?
- Find out how to do a simple science experiment in your kitchen. For example, can you make a volcano cake?

Can You Solve This Logic Puzzle?

Two fathers and two sons made pies for lunch. Each of them baked one pie, but at lunchtime, there were only three pies. No pies were eaten or thrown away. How is this possible?

Are You Good with Words?

Do you love telling stories or jokes? Are you good at reading and writing? Do you find you're good at explaining things to other people? This may mean you have good verbal-linguistic intelligence. You are good at communicating and using language in different ways, either when speaking or writing.

Sasha is a performance poet. That means that she writes poems that are supposed to be performed aloud, rather than read in a book. Sasha loves the sound of words and loves using words that sound like their meaning. Read this poem aloud; which words sound like their meaning?

Last night, I couldn't sleep.
I lay awake
And listened to the sound
The things around
Me make.

The splash of the rain
On my window pane,
The wind's howl,
The screech of an owl,
A dog's growl,

Squeaks and creaks,
Moans and groans,
Bashes and crashes:
Why are sounds louder in your head
Late at night when you're in your bed?

Can You Choose the Correct Words?

- Which word is different from the others:
  control   recover   logic
  support   improve

- Orangutan is to seal as desert is to:
  tree   nest   rainforest
  waterfall   mud

- Which word has a similar meaning to "transform":
  defend   change   reward
  support   process

Improve Your Verbal-Linguistic Intelligence

- Keep a diary and write down things that happen to you or that you think of during the day.
- Give a two-minute talk to your classmates about something you love. Record yourself talking and listen to the playback.
- Play word games or do crossword puzzles.
- Read a lot! Circle any words you don't know and find out what they mean.
- Learn some new jokes and tell them to your friends.

Are You Good at Music?

Do people ever say you have a good sense of rhythm? Are you good at copying sounds you hear around you? Do you like singing or writing your own songs? Can you play one or more musical instruments? You may have a high level of musical intelligence.

Berat is a young musician. He can play four different musical instruments, but his favorite is the cello. He loves the sound of the cello, which he thinks is very emotional. He also thinks it's a very **versatile** instrument—you can play lots of different types of music with the cello. Berat has composed some music for Sasha's poems. They are going to perform together at their next school concert.

Do You Have High Musical Intelligence?

	Yes	No
• Do you like lots of different types of music?	Yes	No
• Do people say you are good at singing?	Yes	No
• Do you find it easy to learn a new song?	Yes	No
• Do you often tap out rhythms?		

Improve Your Musical Intelligence

- Join a band and learn to play a new instrument—it only takes two people to make a band!
- Sing a lot! On your way to school, when you're riding your bike, or when you're taking a shower!
- Listen for rhythms, sounds, or "music" in the world around you—for example, birdsong, the sound of a train going by, or the ticking of the clock in your bedroom.
- Go to concerts and musicals.
- Exchange playlists of music with your friends and listen to new types of music.

Are You Good at Picturing What's Around You?

Do you notice that you're good at finding your way around—even without a map or an app on your phone? Do you like using diagrams and other graphic organizers? Can you picture in your head how a machine works? If so, then you have good spatial intelligence.

People with good spatial intelligence are able to visualize shapes and spaces easily and move them around in their minds. Architects need to have this kind of intelligence because they design buildings and have to visualize the space inside them. This art and media center in Germany was designed by the architect Frank Gehry. There are three separate buildings, which together look like a giant sculpture.

Can You Answer the Questions?

Which group of shapes can be put together to make the shape below?

 a   b c

How many blocks are there in the shape below?

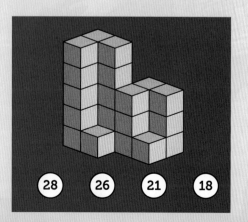

28   26   21   18

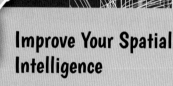

Improve Your Spatial Intelligence

- Use blocks and construction toys to design buildings. Can you think of a new shape for a building?
- Play video games—yes, really! In many games, the action takes place in many different locations that you have to find your way around. In others, you have to create your own spaces.
- Fly a remote-controlled aircraft or drone. When you control the drone, you also have to figure out the direction it is going to take.
- Create a map of your local neighborhood. Make it as detailed as possible.
- Draw every day. What about drawing a famous building from an unusual perspective? Can your friends guess what it is?

Are You Good with People?

Or maybe you're very good with other people. Your friends like talking to you because you listen to them and understand their problems. You notice when other people are sad, and you can cheer them up. If so, then you might have a high level of interpersonal intelligence.

Liam's family moved to a new town recently. He needed to make new friends, so he joined an orienteering club. The club meets in a new location each week. Orienteering is fun, and it's a great way of making friends. An orienteering group has to work together to find its way around. That means listening to each other as well as sharing each member's ideas.

What Would You Do?

Your friend is sad and upset. What do you do?

- Ask your friend what the problem is and try to help.
- Organize a surprise party to distract them.
- Tell them that you're sad, too, and talk about your problems.
- Spend time with someone else that day.

Improve Your Interpersonal Intelligence

- Join a club or start a new hobby that you have to do with other people.
- Make notes with nice things to say to your friends and put them in a jar. Take one note out of the jar each day, and tell a friend!
- Be a good listener. Practice active listening, such as making eye contact or nodding when your friends talk to you.
- Volunteer in your local community. Help others and make new friends!

So what kind of genius are you? Are you a logical-mathematical genius or are you a really good friend? Or do you have a mix of different types of intelligence? Follow the tips here to improve in all ways!

Key Words

1 **Use the Key Words to solve the riddles.**

a My brother is one (some of the time). He spoke five languages when he was nine!

_____

b She does everything and does it quite well. She's really this, and everyone can tell.

_____

c I like hanging out with my friend, Miles. He tells lots of _____ and laughs and smiles.

d You should listen to these, I must insist—all my favorite songs on one long list.

_____

e I looked at it this way and then from that—from two of these, but I just saw a cat.

_____

f Logical, spatial, sometimes musical, good with words, or interpersonal?

_____

Comprehension

2 **Read the sentences and circle *T* (true) or *F* (false).**

a Albert Einstein was good at seeing patterns and making connections between things.   T   F

b All people with verbal-linguistic intelligence are performance poets.   T   F

c If you have a good sense of rhythm, you might have high musical intelligence.   T   F

d People with good spatial intelligence are good at logic puzzles.   T   F

e Good communicators show high levels of interpersonal skills.   T   F

f All geniuses are the same.   T   F

3 **Write the type of intelligence under each skill or activity.**

a John is always singing in the shower or listening to playlists on his headphones.

_____

b Jenny is a good listener. She always cheers me up when I have a problem.

_____

c I'm glad I'm doing my science project with Raheem. He's good at solving problems.

_____

d I want to be an architect when I'm older. I'm good at drawing and design.

_____

e He's always doing crossword puzzles. He even won a crossword competition!

_____

Digging Deeper

4 📖 Read and mark (✔) the main idea of the article.

a You can be a genius if you follow these steps. ☐

b There are different types of intelligence and different ways to improve them. ☐

c Some people are smarter than others. ☐

d You can only improve some types of intelligence. ☐

5 📖 Complete the graphic organizer for the article. Use your ideas from Activity 3 on page 144.

What Kind of Genius Are You?

Before I read the article, I knew that ...	When I read the article, I learned that ..	This gave me this idea:

6 Use ideas from the text to write one piece of advice for each situation.

a Alan always has trouble solving problems in math class.

_____

b Sarah likes listening to new music and is always tapping out rhythms on her desk.

_____

c Fred always has trouble finishing his writing assignments in English class.

_____

d Liz and her family have moved to a new town, and Liz is feeling lonely.

_____

e Katy wants to design a new building for her art class, but she's having trouble visualizing it.

_____

Personalization

7 Choose one type of intelligence you want to improve. List three specific things you can do.

_____

_____

_____

Acknowledgments

The authors and publishers acknowledge the following sources of copyright material and are grateful for the permissions granted. While every effort has been made, it has not always been possible to identify the sources of all the material used or to trace all copyright holders. If any omissions are brought to our notice, we will be happy to include the appropriate acknowledgments on reprinting and in the next update to the digital edition, as applicable.

Key: U = Unit.

Author of the activities: Simon Cupit.

Authors of Nonfiction Texts: **U1:** Keila Ochoa (*Working in the Coldest Place on Earth*); **U2:** Robert Gareth Vaughan (*Getting Out of the Comfort Zone*); **U3:** Kate Fitzgerald (*Art Blog: Why Should You See Art in Person?*); **U5:** Chantal Connaughton (*Take Steps to Reduce Your Carbon Footprint and Save the Planet*).

Photographs

All the photos are sourced from Getty Images.

U1: Sollina Images; Richard Newstead/DigitalVision; PeopleImages/iStock/Getty Images Plus; Tanya Constantine; Caroline Schiff; Zero Creatives/Cultura; Westend61; ONOKY - Eric Audras/Brand X Pictures; Vyacheslav Dumchev/iStock/Getty Images Plus; Jose Luis Pelaez Inc/DigitalVision; Cultura/Publisher Mix; Ascent Xmedia/Stone; Murat Tellioglu/EyeEm; Fabian Plock/EyeEm; CasarsaGuru/E+; Cavan Images; sandsun/iStock/Getty Images Plus; Gary Ellis/EyeEm; Michael Roberts/Moment; Andy Ryan/Stone; Ruben Earth/Moment; VichoT/E+; cunfek/E+; Galen Rowell/Corbis Documentary; Roland Vogel/EyeEm; Artie Photography (Artie Ng)/Moment; piola666/E+; Frans Lemmens/Corbis Unreleased; Brett Phibbs/Image Source; **U2:** Westend61; CiydemImages/iStock/Getty Images Plus; Jetlinerimages/E+; Digital Vision.; Cebas/iStock/Getty Images Plus; Juanmonino/iStock/Getty Images Plus; Mike Powell/Photdisc; SrdjanPav/E+; Hakase_/iStock/Getty Images Plus; Blend Images - Peathegee Inc; Dan Kenyon/Stone; Jovanmandic/iStock/Getty Images Plus; Tonktiti/iStock/Getty Images Plus; Halfdark; SDI Productions/E+; Karol Majewski/Moment; Prostock-Studio/iStock/Getty Images Plus; CarloneGiovanni/iStock Editorial; luckyraccoon/iStock/Getty Images Plus; narvikk/E+; Image Source; john finney photography/Moment; hocus-focus/E+; TravelCouples/Moment; fotoVoyager/E+; Petri Oeschger/Moment; Science Photo Library; Richard Woods/500px/500Px Plus; Constantine Johnny/Moment; Wavebreakmedia/iStock/Getty Images Plus; depic/iStock/Getty Images Plus; JulieanneBirch/E+; stock_colors/E+; Heather E. Binns/Moment; Erik Isakson; Florin Baumann/EyeEm; Photography taken by Mario Gutiérrez./Moment; Michael Roberts/Moment; Michael_Conrad/iStock/Getty Images Plus; **U3:** Flashpop/Stone; Mark Mawson/Stone; Randy Faris/Corbis/VCG; WIN-Initiative/Stone; artpartner-images/The Image Bank; yulkapopkova/E+; Muntz/Taxi/Getty Images Plus; shomos uddin/Moment; Absodels; susaro/iStock/Getty Images Plus; Drypsiak/iStock/Getty Images Plus; Heritage Images/Hulton Fine Art Collection; Ekely/E+; PNC/Digital Vision; Sebastian Leesch/EyeEm; praetorianphoto/E+; Andersen Ross Photography Inc/DigitalVision; Hill Street Studios/DigitalVision; Justin Paget/Stone; Carmen Martínez Torrón/Moment; Patchakorn Phom-in/iStock/Getty Images Plus; kali9/E+; John Turp/Moment; SerhiiBobyk/iStock/Getty Images Plus; Fuse/Corbis; hocus-focus/E+; Frederic Cirou/PhotoAlto Agency RF Collections; oxygen/Moment; Photo Josse/Leemage/Corbis Historical; Fine Art/Corbis Historical; Science Photo Library; Passakorn Leelawat/EyeEm; Cavan Images; RobertoMussi/iStock/Getty Images Plus; Stephanie Hager - HagerPhoto/Stockbyte Unreleased; MediaNews Group/Orange County Register; **U4:** Alina555/E+; Donald Iain Smith; Andrea Colarieti/EyeEm; Prostock-Studio/iStock/Getty Images Plus; Shestock; Peter Cade/Stone; FatCamera/E+; Alan Powdrill/Stone; izusek/iStock/Getty Images Plus; Caroline Schiff; esolla/iStock/Getty Images Plus; XiXinXing; REB Images; mikkelwilliam/E+; pictafolio/E+; Cultura RF/Tim Hall; tadamichi/iStock/Getty Images Plus; Neustockimages/E+; Deagreez/iStock/Getty Images Plus; InspirationGP/iStock/Getty Images Plus; JGI/Jamie Grill; GeorgiosArt/iStock/Getty Images Plus; nazar_ab/iStock/Getty Images Plus; hakule/DigitalVision Vectors; Dong Wenjie/Moment; Nipitphon Na Chiangmai/EyeEm; metamorworks/iStock/Getty Images Plus; Alex Potemkin/E+; Jose Luis Pelaez/Photodisc; **U5:** Rawpixel/iStock/Getty Images Plus; MILATAS; Jose Luis Pelaez Inc/DigitalVision; pidjoe/E+; tbd/E+; Esther Moreno Martinez/EyeEm; VichienPetchmai/iStock/Getty Images Plus; AleksandarGeorgiev/E+; Ljupco/iStock/Getty Images Plus; Richard Drury/DigitalVision; PhotoAlto/Odilon Dimier/PhotoAlto Agency RF Collections; p_ponomareva/iStock/Getty Images Plus; mikroman6/Moment; Ascent/PKS Media Inc./Stone; Guasor/iStock/Getty Images Plus; Capelle.r/Moment; Xvision/Moment; Maskot; Daniel Grizelj/DigitalVision; Dougal Waters/Digital Vision; Abdul Raheem Mohamed/EyeEm; Robin Meurer/EyeEm; Nattawun Wimonpon/EyeEm; Jacobs Stock Photography Ltd/

DigitalVision; powerofforever/E+; Ricardo Lima/Moment; Sam Barnes/Moment; Paolo Paradiso/iStock/Getty Images Plus; PeopleImages/E+; AleksandarNakic/E+; Rosemary Calvert/Stone; istetiana/Moment; Photographer/iStock/Getty Images Plus; Claudio Rampinini/iStock/Getty Images Plus; katleho Seisa/E+; izusek/E+; Roberto Westbrook; FatCamera/iStock/Getty Images Plus; Liam Norris/Cultura; fotograzia/Moment; Perkus/E+; Nattawun Wimonpon/EyeEm; **U6:** Alexander Spatari/Moment; uschools/E+; Jose Luis Pelaez Inc/DigitalVision; Paul Taylor/Stone; Jeffrey Coolidge/DigitalVision; Vladimir Serov; Klaus Vedfelt/DigitalVision; Carl Lyttle/The Image Bank; Anthony Tulliani/EyeEm; John Lund/Stone; Arx0nt/Moment; Page Light Studios/iStock/Getty Images Plus; Anton Smirnov/iStock/Getty Images Plus; DNY59/E+; Nicola Tree/Stone; arsenik/E+; Polina Panna/iStock/Getty Images Plus; Robert Niedring/Alloy; JackF/iStock/Getty Images Plus; Jessica Graham/Imagezoo; InnaBodrova/DigitalVision Vectors; memoangeles/iStock/Getty Images Plus; fotograzia/Moment; Sergey Ryumin/Moment; George/Moment; sam thomas/iStock/Getty Images Plus; Digital Vision; id-work/DigitalVision Vectors; Katsumi Murouchi/Moment; jayk7/Moment; Richard Wear; Westend61; myillo/DigitalVision Vectors; Ceneri/DigitalVision Vectors; duncan1890/DigitalVision Vectors; JillianSuzanne/iStock/Getty Images Plus; Image Source/Photodisc; Steve Sparrow/Cultura; Big_Ryan/DigitalVision Vectors; **U7:** BJI/Blue Jean Images; ChesiireCat/iStock/Getty Images Plus; Holloway/Stone; SeventyFour/iStock/Getty Images Plus; LightFieldStudios/iStock/Getty Images Plus; skynesher/E+; fStop Images; Jose Luis Pelaez Inc/DigitalVision; CR Productions Limited/DigitalVision; jaroon/E+; Goldmund/iStock/Getty Images Plus; Design Cells/iStock/Getty Images Plus; Marilyn Nieves/E+; dolphfyn/iStock/Getty Images Plus; Ca-ssis/iStock/Getty Images Plus; Monty Rakusen/Cultura; Mint Images/Art Wolfe/Mint Images RF; Adene Sanchez/E+; Jupiterimages/Pixland; Sylvain Sonnet/The Image Bank Unreleased; Sinhyu/iStock/Getty Images Plus; Alfred Eisenstaedt/The LIFE Picture Collection; Science Photo Library - SCIEPRO/Brand X Pictures; FotografiaBasica/E+; martin-dm/E+; poba/E+; OsakaWayne Studios/Moment; Nur Wahit/EyeEm; Cavan Images; gradyreese/E+; Rodolfo Parulan Jr./Moment; seksan Mongkhonkhamsao/Moment; Jacobs Stock Photography/Photodisc; Rafe Swan/Cultura; **U8:** Prostock-Studio/iStock/Getty Images Plus; Portra/DigitalVision; Robert Niedring/MITO images; JGI/Jamie Grill; Cavan Images; Daniel Grill; Sneksy/iStock/Getty Images Plus; Deagreez/iStock/Getty Images Plus; John M Lund Photography Inc/Stone; vejaa/iStock/Getty Images Plus; Tetra Images; Ana Maria Serrano/Moment; Richard Sharrocks/Moment; Compassionate Eye Foundation/Digitalvision; pidjoe/iStock/Getty Images Plus; matthiashaas/iStock/Getty Images Plus; Ilona Nagy/Moment; Adam Smigielski/E+; Tek Image/Science Photo Library; fivepointsix/iStock/Getty Images Plus; Burcu Atalay Tankut/Moment; resavac/iStock/Getty Images Plus; John Seaton Callahan/Moment; josefkubes/iStock/Getty Images Plus; Mieszko9/iStock/Getty Images Plus; mikroman6/Moment; Chuanchai Pundej/EyeEm; Achmad Arphan/EyeEm; Image Source; Busakorn Pongparnit/Moment; **U9:** Glasshouse Images/The Image Bank; Image Source; Thomas Northcut/Photodisc; Life On White/Photodisc; ChooChin/iStock/Getty Images Plus; appletat/iStock/Getty Images Plus; Evgenii Mitroshin/iStock Editorial; Nirut Saelim/EyeEm; jeangill/E+; Deagreez/iStock/Getty Images Plus; twinsterphoto/iStock/Getty Images Plus; Hill Street Studios/DigitalVision; draganab/iStock/Getty Images Plus; Artur Debat/Moment; Steven Puetzer/Photographer's Choice RF; Kwanchai Lerttanapunyaporn/EyeEm; AVIcons/iStock/Getty Images Plus; LightFieldStudios/iStock/Getty Images Plus; shuoshu/DigitalVision Vectors; fotostorm/E+; VikramRaghuvanshi/E+; Lambert/Hulton Archive; cnythzl/DigitalVision Vectors; kyoshino/E+; hanapon1002/iStock/Getty Images Plus; Jose Girarte/E+; Will & Deni McIntyre/Corbis Documentary; FrankRamspott/DigitalVision Vectors; DragonImages/iStock/Getty Images Plus; desifoto/DigitalVision Vectors; filo/DigitalVision Vectors; imageBROKER/Rolf Fischer; Miguel Sotomayor/Moment Open; nadla/E+; Shannon Fagan/Photodisc; SDI Productions/E+; Jobalou/DigitalVision Vectors; Andyd/E+.

Illustrations

Berenice Muñiz; Emmanuel Urueta; Ismael Vázquez; Israel Ramírez; Kathia Recio; Marco Antonio Reyes; Mario Garza; Ricardo Figueroa; Richard Zela; Tania Juárez.

Cover Artwork commissioned by Aphik S.A. de C.V.

Cover Illustration by Mario Garza.

Page make-up

Aphik S.A. de C.V.

Audio recording

Audio recording by CityVox.